7 DEADLY DISEASES OF MINISTRY MARKETING

Confessions of a Christian Fundraiser

by Doug Brendel

with E. Dale Berkey, Ph.D. & Jack W. Sheline

THE 7 DEADLY DISEASES OF MINISTRY MARKETING
Confessions of a Christian Fundraiser

published by International Christian Publishers

© 1998 Berkey Brendel Sheline

Printed in the United States of America

International Standard Book Number: 1890525-24-3

Cover design by: J. David Ford & Associates
Hurst, Texas

BERKEY BRENDEL SHELINE
Ministry Development Specialists
60 Shiawassee, Suite G • Fairlawn, OH 44333
voice (330) 867-5224 • fax (330) 869-5607 • email servant@servantheart.com
www.servantheart.com

"This is an excellent expression of the sometimes-difficult truth about fundraising for Christian ministries! It's fun to read but also relentlessly honest. I imagine many who work inside Christian organizations will pass the book along to the marketing decision-makers because it says things they don't have the nerve to!"

—Matt Krepcho, Vice-President for Communications
Coral Ridge Ministries

"What a gift! To get these insights in book form will be a huge help to countless ministries. I've worked with the authors for 20 years, and I've seen firsthand how these principles perform in real life. Every member of our ministry's fundraising team — and every member of our board — is going to get a copy of this book from me!"

—Bob Hoskins, Founder
Book of Life International

"Thank God that Brendel employed such disarming wit to administer such strong medicine! This is not just about getting fundraising right — it's about getting my Christian walk right. A surprising and challenging book."

—The Rev. Todd Wetzel, Executive Director
Episcopalians United

"I have known and worked with the Berkey Brendel Sheline partners for years, and it's more than just a working relationship; we've become friends. Along the way, I have seen for myself that the principles in this book work!"

—Rod Parsley, Pastor
World Harvest Church

"Our ministry has a ten-year history of creating fundraising strategies with Berkey Brendel Sheline. They have demonstrated to me that the truths expressed in this book apply to college recruitment, television broadcasting, direct mail, the marketing of ministry products, and the list goes on."

—Dr. Jerry Falwell, Chancellor
Liberty University

Table of Contents

Introduction

AUTOPSIES FIRST

No, this ain't a deli.

We're a "ministry to ministries."

We help ministries grow.

We're called Berkey Brendel Sheline — which, according to a friend of mine, *sounds* like a deli.

Well, sorry. It's just our names.

Over the past decade and a half, we've had the privilege of serving about 100 ministries — large and small, rich and poor, famous and invisible — in just about every imaginable type of work. We've served alongside Christian churches, colleges, humanitarian organizations, publishers and literature distributors, media producers and broadcasters, and the list goes on.

I wish I could say that my brilliant creativity combined with Dale Berkey's superior wisdom and Jack Sheline's outstanding insight magically resulted in flawless marketing strategies for every single one of our clients.

But that would be a massive fib.

The truth is that we've often had to learn the hard way.

Sometimes I've actually had the feeling that the success of a ministry fundraising strategy is inversely proportionate to the confidence with which you launch it. Just when you think things are going along swimmingly, you suddenly find yourself flopping on the beach.

I would have to say that, in one way or another, at one time or another, we have suffered all seven of the

Seven Deadly Diseases of Ministry Marketing.

On the other hand, we've kept careful notes. We share a passion for God's work, and we hate to fail. So, in an effort to avoid encountering *more* failures, we dissect each flop, analyze it, map it — like Richard Dreyfuss in *Jaws*, gasping at the stench and horror of it. Whatever it takes to elude failure's ugly face the *next* time!

And as a result of such ardent effort (unfortunately, we did quite a number of dissections in the early days), we've learned a few things.

We'd like to share them.

We'd like for your ministry to succeed — to thrive — by learning these lessons the *easy* way. It's disheartening to imagine your ministry squandering its resources on mistakes that *we've* already made ... simply because it's so *unnecessary*. We've already done the dissection; why should you have to hold your nose?

Of course, some things are easier smelled than done. You may feel some ill ease as you read this book. Some of the concepts we've discovered are so upside-down from "common wisdom" that even *we* feel uneasy. In many ways, the truth about how you market your ministry reveals some truth about yourself, and particularly your *view* of yourself. That can be an uncomfortable discovery.

On the other hand, we've had the joy of seeing many, many churches and ministries grow healthy and strong by employing these hard-learned principles. Sometimes they've been employed reluctantly at first, and embraced skeptically ... but that may actually be the sweetest kind of success: the kind you thought you'd probably never have.

Is this all too scary? Fear not. Let me offer two

assurances which I trust will fortify your confidence enough to plunge ahead and read with an open mind:

1. Christ calls us *not* to be His lawyers, arguing His case to the world, but simply His *witnesses* (Acts 1:8), describing what happened in our lives as a result of meeting Him. Taking Christ's instructions for evangelism as a model, this book will only tell you what we've experienced — what we've seen, what we've done, what has actually happened. Wherever this is not the case, I'll carefully note otherwise. This is not a book of philosophy, nor is it an essay designed to persuade. It's just the testimony of witnesses: Dale Berkey, Doug Brendel, Jack Sheline, and our associates. So you can have complete confidence that what you have is *evidence*, not just *theory*.

2. Your Bible has 66 books in it. Not 67. There is no Book of Marketing. There's a reason for this. The principles by which ministries are to market themselves are not separate from the principles by which we minister. Nor are the principles by which we minister separate from the principles by which we *live our lives*. God created people to interact according to a wonderfully enriching design. Wherever we don't align with the design by which God created us, there's going to be a sense of disquiet. First Peter 1:15 calls us to holiness in *all* we do. There is no footnote excusing or excluding ministry marketing personnel.

So to the best of our ability, Dale and Jack and I have based the contents of this book on the principles of Scripture. Sometimes it would have been easier to wink at Scripture — Jesus went ballistic in the temple, for example (John 2:16), and yelled "How dare you turn my

Father's house into a *market!*" Chilling words for people involved in *marketing.* Still, we've relentlessly returned to the pages of Scripture to determine whether our observations in the real-life marketplace fully square with the blueprint of God's Word. I'll show you what we discovered — the good, the bad, and the confusing.

If God has called you into any kind of ministry, we salute you — and we pray for you. As Bill Hybels has observed, you didn't deserve your leadership gift ... you didn't earn it, you didn't purchase it. God simply chose you for it. But now that you have this leadership gift, you have the responsibility to invest it wisely. It's a weighty responsibility. How you deal with it has enormous consequences — in this life and in eternity. Our prayer is that you will achieve the total potential that God dreamed up for you. We hope and pray that God will see fit to make this book a means to that end.

Since most of our work has been with "parachurch" ministries, I've focused most of the book on these organizations that "come alongside." But the principles are truly transferable to the local church. The more they're applied to the church leader's relationship with his or her parishioners, the greater the potential for success of a truly spiritual kind.

If you want to dialogue about more specific ways to adapt these principles for use in your local church, email us via servant@servantheart.com. Or email me personally via brendel@servantheart.com. We welcome your questions, and your feedback.

* * * * *

Okay, they're not actually *diseases*.

I call them the Seven Deadly Diseases of Ministry Marketing because — well, they *are* deadly. Do any one of them, and you're certain to kill some portion of your ministry potential.

I originally wanted to call it "The Seven Deadly *Sins* of Ministry Marketing." In a way, breaking any of these "rules" is just like sinning. The biblical word *sin* is an archery term. It indicates a falling short of the target. God designed you a certain way; you don't measure up. Romans 3:23 turns out to be true! "All have sinned and fall short ...." You fall short not only of His ideal, but of your potential. You break God's heart — because you can't achieve as fully the rich, rewarding agenda He scheduled for you.

Likewise, these Seven Deadly "Sins" of Ministry Marketing represent the most common ways in which ministries fall short of their potential. Every ministry falls short in some way. (Hey, there's Romans 3:23 again.) No organization is perfect. But you still want to avoid sin as much as possible — since the more you sin, the shorter you fall.

Am I saying that whatever advice you get from Berkey Brendel Sheline is godly, and whenever you disagree with us, you've made yourself a rank sinner?

Nope. And so — in hopes of avoiding any misunderstanding — we'll call them the Seven Deadly *Diseases* of Ministry Marketing. Even godly people get sick — and even good ministries have marketing diseases.

To be sure, we don't have all the answers for interpreting the Seven Deadly Diseases of Ministry Marketing for a given ministry operation. There are millions of decisions to be made about how to think and live and work within the framework of the "rules" we'll be expressing. That's the tricky part: the *application* to *your ministry* — the part where God's Spirit and your God-given instincts and years of hard-knocks experience must come into play.

But the basic Deadly Diseases are known; they are recognizable — and they are based on bottom-line, bedrock truths. Learn these truths, think and live and work by them, and you have a strong chance of moving closer to God's ideal for yourself and your ministry. Your ministry gets healthier. Ignore these truths, think and live and work by some other code, and you are likely to move away from God's ideal for yourself and your ministry. Your ministry gets sicker.

As Ross Perot might say, "It's as simple as that."

* * * * *

On the other hand, as Paul Harvey might say, "Here's the rest of the story."

The wonderful thing about these marketing diseases — okay, maybe wonderful is too strong a word — is that they can be cured. In our ministry marketing programs, we can always change course — and come closer to our potential. (If we were talking about "sins," we could talk about being "redeemed.")

All we have to be is willing.

But the horrible thing about disease — okay, there are *lots* of horrible things about disease, but one of the *worst* things about disease is that even if you get well, you've still suffered ... and you may still have to suffer the after-effects of the illness.

I had a friend who came to Christ after many years of sexual immorality and drug abuse. Christ totally cleansed him, justified him, and received him — but my friend still died of AIDS.

Sadly, the same is true of ministry organizations. When they catch one or more of the Seven Deadly Diseases of Ministry Marketing, they plant poisonous seeds in their own fields. The sin analogy applies. Plant a "little" sin — reap a little suffering. Plant tons of sin — look out, you're in big trouble.

Sometimes a good Christian organization will successfully avoid six of the Seven Deadly Diseases of Ministry Marketing, but continue in *just one of them.* They usually have what seems to be a reasonable rationale. "All that other stuff is okay," they say, in effect, "but in this area, we know better." Or, "Our donors are different." Or, most frequently, "That's just not *us.*"

In any case, an organization harms itself in the same proportion by which it fails to square with the biblical ideal. God designed the universe this way, and the challenge for ministry organizations is the same as the challenge for individuals: Be like Jesus. Ask the now-popular question "WWJD?" — What Would Jesus Do?

For example: Frankly, I don't like the idea of Proverbs 15:1 — "A gentle answer turns away wrath, but a harsh word stirs up anger." That's just not *me.* By nature, I'm more of a harsh-answer guy. But that doesn't change the truth of Proverbs 15:1. Here's a case where I need to be less like *me,* and more like *Jesus.*

Likewise, ministries sometimes need to change their fundraising strategies. Not just for change's sake, but for the sake of conforming to the biblical blueprint. They need to become less like *themselves*, more like the One in whose name they serve.

Dale and Jack and I love ministries. We love the people who work in ministries. It's not just the love of a common commitment; it's genuine affection. We like them! Our hearts beat alike. Yet with that affection comes occasional sadness. We hurt when we see ministries facing difficult choices — but we also hurt when we see a ministry's potential going unfulfilled because the difficult choice hasn't been made. In a way, we feel like the prodigal's father in Luke 15, eager to see the ministry thrive, willing to help however the ministry is willing to be helped, grieving when the error has produced unnecessary loss.

But when truth conquers — when the hard choices are made, and the fruit begins to emerge — that's a time of celebration for us, a time of joy. It's exhilarating to see a ministry moving *toward*, not away from, its full potential for the cause of Christ ... and that *more*, not less, of its God-given mission will be accomplished.

Down through the years we've had the joy of working with a tense, troubled ministry team and one day seeing "the light go on" and the delight of serving God return ... the joy of seeing a struggling ministry turn the corner and begin to accelerate and make an unprecedented impact ... the joy of wrangling a seemingly impossible tangle of problems into a streamlined, super-effective force for the cause of Christ. In every victory, as we thank God for His grace, we observe once again that His most profound work began when the ministry team embraced His direction and design. This book is our best effort to reflect what we've observed to be His design for His work ... which we want to be *our* work!

We are humbled that God would give us the privilege of serving so many ministries, and we are grateful for the opportunity to spend the next few pages with you. Our prayer is that they will be profitable for you, and for the Kingdom.

Chapter 1

DEADLY DISEASE #1: AMNESIA

Who am I? What am I?
What am I doing here? Why?

William Powell was the charming, dapper, sophisticated man-about-town of the *Thin Man* movies in the 1930's and 40's.

Unfortunately, he made a few clunkers along the way. Like I *Love You Again* with Myrna Loy.

In this long-forgotten almost-a-comedy, Powell plays a no-good, two-timing con man who gets konked on the head and wakes up with total amnesia.

Hasn't a clue who he is.

So he proceeds to become a fragile, effete goody-two-shoes, a civic booster, and model citizen. Not to mention an industrious business owner who makes a fortune and faithfully gives tons of it to charity.

Until, that is — he gets konked on the head again, and ....

Well, you can see why I *Love You Again* didn't go down in history alongside *Casablanca* and *Gone With the Wind*.

But William Powell's problem in that lame I *Love You Again* movie is, in an important way, the same as the problem of many ministries today.

They don't really know who they are. Couldn't tell you if they tried.

This may seem like a harsh, extreme statement — we find ourselves reflexively responding with "That certainly doesn't apply to *my* ministry!" — until a visitor wanders through the halls of our ministry facility and asks each employee this simple question:

What is this ministry all about?

Try it sometime. Find a neighbor or acquaintance who's never visited your ministry operations site. Some man or woman whom the ministry's employees don't already know. Send this stranger on a mission. If you have a James Bond sense of adventure, wire him with a secret tape recorder. If your style is more along the lines of, say, Chevy Chase, just give the visitor a little handheld unit and have him record his encounters in plain sight.

Then sit down in a secluded place, take a deep breath, and listen to the tape.

You may need an Advil.

> In the best and most effective ministry organizations, most employees are able to articulate the mission of the ministry to a stranger.

If the tape of *your* ministry employees features halting, confused, maybe even erroneous "mission statements," you're not alone. But you do have work to do — because those employees are the people shaping the work of your ministry from the lowest level of your organizational chart on up.

And that same bewilderment strongly influences — *skews* would be a more accurate term — the message you communicate to your donors.

What is your ministry all about?

Can you articulate "The Message" in a single sentence? In three sentences? In three minutes?

Dr. Darryl DelHousaye, senior pastor of Arizona's Scottsdale Bible Church, urges each member of his congregation to come up with the story of his or her conversion to Christ — but in a three-minute format. This allows the believer to share his testimony in virtually any setting, whenever the opportunity arises.

The same tactic would be valuable for any ministry organization. If every employee and volunteer involved in your ministry could tell a total stranger what your ministry is "all about" in three minutes flat, you would have a unified corps of workers focusing on a single long-term goal.

Of course, it's not that simple. Those are probably the most difficult three minutes you'll ever engineer.

In most ministries, we have found the process of determining the "message" to be arduous, even painful. Where we have challenged a ministry staff to develop a firm message, members of the leadership team often find that they suddenly turn into the Continental Congress of 1776 — differing over concepts and wordings and meanings that they never before realized they differed on, and unable to agree on a unified declaration. In a surprising number of cases, the ministry "principal" — the most public personality leading the ministry — actually has a different take on expressing the organization's mission than the staff does. It's a disorienting discovery ...

but it's enormously important to go through. The ministry can become dramatically healthier when such dissonance is revealed and dealt with.

Yet even after you've got your entire ministry team on the same page — even after your mission is crystal-clear — there still usually remains one major problem:

The message may actually make no sense to your target audience!

* * * * *

In order to determine "The Message" for your ministry, it's crucial to understand what "The Message" is *not*.

It's easy to confuse the concept of the message with the concept of the mission statement — or even an operational blueprint. "The Message" of the ministry can't be a multi-page document detailing everything the ministry does. "The Message" of the ministry also can't be a paragraph so long and involved and confusing that it can only be interpreted by a veteran staff member.

Certainly an organization can use documents like these *internally*, as a guide for workers.

But your message has to be *donor-edible*.

If I can gobble up your message — if I can see it, want it, reach out and grab it, pop it, chew it up and swallow it, all within about eight seconds — then I may want to eat some more of what you're cooking. You've offered me a donor-edible message, and I am grateful!

But if I have to study your message — if it makes me furrow my brow, like a five-year-old contemplating fried mushrooms — if I have to contemplate it, figure it

out, sniff it warily, cut it with a knife and fork, or
otherwise process it ... well, then, I may as well have
cooked for myself — and I am very, very unlikely to want
more of whatever this stuff was that you offered me.

What is your ministry all about? Compare your
answer to a few of these good message statements:

* "We help poor kids in Latin America by
    getting them in school, giving them meals,
    clothing them, giving them medical care, and
    teaching them all about Jesus."

* "We take people who have given up on
    church and connect them to the life-changing
    power of a thriving relationship with Jesus
    Christ."

* "We reclaim run-down neighborhoods by
    offering inner-city people food, job training,
    and other helps, and then leading them to
    faith in Christ."

* "We help public school students learn about
    God's 'Intelligent Design' in science and history
    instead of just evolution and secularism."

* "We use TV to teach people to live by the
    practical truths of the Scripture."

I sympathize when ministry leaders feel
uncomfortable about reducing their mission to a single
message. It can be unnerving to think that anybody could

express their work — to which they are giving their entire lives — in just one breath. But look at Jesus, who willingly rose to the challenge in Matthew 22:35-40 when a lawyer asked Him to narrow it all down for him. He hung "all the Law and the Prophets" on just two commandments. (Was Moses watching from heaven? He must have been fidgeting!) Paul boils it down even further, in Romans 13:10: "... Love is the fulfillment of the law."

A single mission message does not have to imply simplicity or a lack of value. The Westminster Confession states that the *purpose of life* — this is the purpose of life we're talking about, now! — is simply to "glorify God and enjoy Him forever." That's clear, concise, bold, and profound — yet we struggle a lifetime to answer much smaller questions!

Regardless of our natural discomfort with the idea, the boiling-down of a ministry into a single message is essential — and more so each year, as our culture whirls into more and more frenzied chaos.

This was the concept perfectly understood, and executed, by the now-famous James Carville — the bald, foul-mouthed Cajun-French good ol' boy who ran the "War Room" that brought Bill Clinton to the presidency in 1992. The over-arching strategy of that first Clinton campaign was expressed in the hand-drawn sign that Carville tacked up in Clinton's campaign headquarters. You've read about this, probably more than once: the sign simply said, "The economy, stupid." Carville insisted that the message of the campaign was nothing more or less than "The economy is broken, and Bill Clinton can fix it."

Of course, the economy may or may not have been

broken. And no President has even the *legal* power, let alone the intelligence, to actually *fix* a whole *economy*, for heaven's sake!

But as far as James Carville was concerned, truth wasn't necessarily the point.

The point was to *persuade* the voters.

And the most effective technique for accomplishing that persuasion was, as Carville realized, *not* to tell them everything about every subject. *Not* to fritter the days away answering charges about old girlfriends and draft-dodging hijinks. But rather to narrow the message to a single thought, something people *care* about, and then repeat it and repeat it and repeat it and repeat it and repeat it and repeat it and repeat it and repeat it and repeat it and repeat it and repeat it and repeat it and repeat it.

Are the American people idiots? No. But they are busy. They are distracted. They are living under the tyranny of the urgent. Right now they are doing what seems to be important *right now* — changing Justin's diaper or balancing the checkbook or calling the cops about the neighbor's noisy dog — so if a message is going to get through to their brain, it's going to have to come at them an enormous number of times, with extreme consistency and clarity. And it's going to have to be something that matters to *them*.

George Bush himself pouted that he somehow just "didn't connect with the voters." That assessment was exactly, perfectly correct. But that connection could not happen solely through campaign *techniques* — spots on TV, rallies in stadiums, full-color mailings, whatever. *Connection* is a human thing, not a mechanical thing. It relies more on the message than the mechanics of the communication.

Now, with Christ's own example (and Carville's strategy) as background, what about you and the mission of your organization?

When it comes to asking your donors for help, you must "stay on message."

You certainly want to tell the truth. But you also want to persuade your "voters." Yours may be a superb ministry, with great programs and creative fundraising strategies. But if you're not getting enough response from your target audience, it may be because your messages to them are all over the map. In today's frenzied marketplace, with a zillion messages zinging through every donor's life every day, the organizations communicating Carville-style are the ones getting response.

So — bottom line: You'll need a message.

But not just any message.

A message that communicates the *unique* mission of your ministry.

How? Here are guidelines:

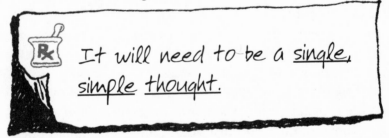

> **Rx** It will need to be a <u>single, simple</u> <u>thought.</u>

Many Christian organizations have a bunch of stuff to say, and they say most or all of it in every communication to their donors. They do not communicate a single, simple message. The busy donor can't focus: *What do you want me to* DO? she asks silently, poised over the garbage can as she reads her mail. Even if your ministry is wonderfully effective, if you're not successful in communicating your mission to your donor, she can't help you as much as she otherwise might.

> ℞ Your message will need to be something you can live with for a long time, because you will need to <u>communicate</u> it <u>to</u> <u>your</u> <u>donor</u> <u>frequently</u>.

It's our natural tendency to think of our donors as a great stagnant pool of people, lying still and solemn, next to the mailbox, with nothing to disturb their solitude but the mail they receive from charities. This thinking motivates us as a ministry organization to ask for help less often — and then to "vary the request" from mailing to mailing.

But donors are not hovering near the mailbox, waiting breathlessly for the next communication from us.

They are busy and distracted: they have grandkids tearing up the house, they have supper to cook and no shortening in the cupboard, they have this funny little pain in the shoulder — is this bursitis again, or something new? The donor's life is *not* that stagnant pond, where your fundraising letter drops like a rock to make enormous, beautiful ripples. The donor's life is a raging, chaotic river, where your fundraising letter hardly makes a *blup!* on the surface before it disappears — actually in something between 8 and 14 seconds. The average donor doesn't dread an organization's appeals because she doesn't *think* about the organization *at all* during the time between appeals. Most donors don't track the frequency of appeals nearly as accurately as they track the *message* of those appeals.

> **℞** your message must be expressed in <u>terms the donor understands.</u>

We must not talk to our donors like a neurosurgeon at a neurosurgery conference — in clinical, unemotional terminology. We need to communicate in the language that regular everyday people understand and use. If we communicate in cool, corporate terms, the distracted donor doesn't hear anything that makes her heart go *thump* and inspires her to stop a moment and consider the appeal.

You can't talk to a human being like a corporation — even if you *are* a corporation. You must talk like a warm, personable human being.

> # your message **must** **count** to the donor.

This is the toughest nut to crack in the process of ministry development, and it has to be re-thought with each new communication with the donor. Your message will be presented many times, in many varied forms — mail, phone, video, audio, print, in person — with countless different "spins" or approaches. And every single time, the issue of *why this should matter to the donor* must be settled all over again.

Many Christian organizations innocently communicate messages about which the donor doesn't care in the slightest. Every detail of your operation is important to you, and you earnestly *want* every detail of your operation to be important to your donors. This is natural. But the harsh truth is, most donors will find most details of your operation *boring*.

You also want to think of your donors as high-minded, selfless loyalists — but in fact most will have to perceive some benefit to *themselves* in order to respond to your appeal ... even if the only benefit is an improved feeling about themselves.

The toughest challenge for any charitable ministry is to figure out a connection to the donor — something that is truly *about* the ministry, but also somehow *about* the donor.

Many Christian organizations spend a disproportionate chunk of their resources on the mechanics of asking for money — without having refined the message which *absolutely must drive every request for funds.*

Secular charities are generally better at this. One day I was slowing at a red light when a vast shadow fell across the earth, and I looked up to see that a semi-truck had pulled into the lane next to me. On the side of the semi was a logo: American Red Cross. What could the American Red Cross need a semi for? A semi is big and slow. Everybody knows the Red Cross is speedy. In a disaster, they're the first ones there.

Of course, there are lots of reasons why the American Red Cross might need a semi. But none sprang to mind as I sat at that red light. Why not?

Because the American Red Cross has engaged in extremely intelligent marketing.

We don't know they have semis full of who-knows-what because they've never told us.

Instead, they've spent decades telling us just one thing: In a disaster, the Red Cross gets there first.

They've built a massive, complex humanitarian organization out of that tiny little sliver of a thought.

They've asked millions of Americans for money millions of times, largely through the mail. I estimate that I alone have received a quarter-million letters from them. But they've never once asked me to give to help them buy or repair their semis. They've never asked me to help them train body dogs to search disaster debris. They've never asked me to make up the shortfall in President Elizabeth Dole's salary. They've never asked me to contribute money so they could establish their state-of-the-art blood system, a triumph of modern science which now provides half of America's blood supply. I've never been solicited to underwrite the Annual Red Cross Award, or the Annual Red Cross Award Dinner Dance where they give it away.

All I've been asked to do is give so when there's a disaster, the Red Cross can get there first.

We in ministry desperately need to learn this simple but crucial lesson. We have wonderfully complicated, multi-faceted ministries, and we need loads of money to keep them going. But we make the mistake of going to our donors and *telling them all about it.*

We explain the nuts and bolts. We reveal the rationale.

We outline our outreaches, spell out our systems, chart our course — offering the donor a dazzling array of detail.

Detail which, unfortunately, only our ministry's leadership finds fascinating.

The donor, meanwhile, has already dropped the letter into the garbage and moved on to the latest issue of *Better Homes & Gardens* or *Sports Illustrated.*

Certainly major donors to any ministry have a much higher tolerance for detail, maybe even a *need* for deeper levels of information. But the vast majority of a ministry's donors are not as tuned in to the details of our cause as we would love to believe.

This is why our agency preaches the gospel of narrowing a ministry's message to a single, laser-beam-like thought, and then hammering home that same message again and again, in every appeal letter. Never explaining another thrilling ministry strategy. Never mucking up an appeal letter with another inspiring message on why we do what we do. But simply telling story after story of people whose lives were touched and transformed because of the ministry's unique ability to do whatever it is the ministry does.

A simple strategy, but oh so difficult to accomplish, when we yearn to tell our donors everything we know! (If only they were as engrossed in the minutiae of our work as we are! But then, if they were, they'd probably have our jobs. And then where would we be?)

Have you clarified the message of your ministry?

Do it.

Squeeze your message. Squash it. When you squeeze a grape, you get wine. Squeeze fruit, you get nectar. Squeeze a rose, you get perfume. Squeeze a lump of coal — you get a diamond!

Squeeze your message, squash it, whittle away at it, until it's one sentence — one thought — which communicates the very essence of your mission.

A message that matters to donors. A message that can be easily understood.

> *A message you can live with month after month after month, in everything you say, everything you do, everything you print and mail.*

Then the challenge becomes *how* to bring that message before busy, distracted donors so that it *connects* with them right where they are. As Paul says in Ephesians 4:29, "[Say] only what is helpful for building others up *according to their needs*, that it may *benefit those who listen*."

In our offices we display a poster — and we have sent a copy to each of the ministries we serve — which serves as our hopefully-more-pleasant version of that obnoxious sign that James Carville hung up for his staff. It's included here, and I recommend that you post it somewhere in your offices, too — someplace where it can be seen, and read, and absorbed.

Absorb this principle — live by it, work by it, make it part of everything you do — and maybe you won't need two konks on the head, like William Powell did, before you can tell folks who you are!

BERKEY BRENDEL SHELINE

The Message

is more important than the mechanics
of communicating it.

The Message

must compete with thousands of
other matters intruding on the
donor's attention.

The Message

therefore must be repeated constantly,
in terms that the donors understand,
and in ways that make it count
for them.

Ministry Development Specialists
www.servantheart.com

Chapter 2

DEADLY DISEASE #2: SCHIZOPHRENIA

I'm okay, and so am I

I serve as a teaching pastor at Mountain Valley Community Church in Scottsdale, Arizona, and as we write this book I am in the middle of a miserable, wonderful series of sermons.

What could I have been thinking when I decided to walk our congregation of mostly young-in-Christ believers through all the "words in red" in their Bibles — the words of Jesus?

The problem isn't that Jesus said a *lot* of things, and this series is going to take *years.*

And the problem isn't that Jesus had nothing interesting or helpful to say. The truth is that many of our studies have been amazing — thrilling — life-changing — because Jesus was a phenomenal communicator.

The problem is that Jesus also said a bunch of things I'd rather not teach.

As Philip Yancey has so eloquently complained in his book *The Jesus I Never Knew,* our actual Lord is a far cry from the mellow, stained-glass Jesus of our Sunday schools and storybooks.

I really wish, for example, that the Apostle John had conveniently failed to record that whole nasty encounter in the temple (John 2:14-17 NIV):

> In the temple courts he found men selling
> cattle, sheep and doves, and others sitting at
> tables exchanging money.
> So he made a whip out of cords, and drove all
> from the temple area, both sheep and cattle; he
> scattered the coins of the money changers and
> overturned their tables.
> To those who sold doves he said, "Get these
> out of here! How dare you turn my Father's house
> into a market!"
> His disciples remembered that it is written:
> "Zeal for your house will consume me."

I'd like to rationalize that all Jesus really meant to
say was that we shouldn't sell books and tapes in our
church foyers.

But something deep inside me says that's not the
idea.

On one hand, we can look at Jesus' cleansing of the
temple as symbolic. The Lamb of God had come; the old
rituals of animal sacrifice would no longer be needed.

On the other hand, He didn't stop there.

He had to go one step further.

It's that very direct and unconditional use of the
word *market* that makes me the most nervous. At least the
old King James Version translated it *house of merchandise*;
that was easier to reconcile with my line of work —
marketing ministries!

When Jesus twisted those leather strips into a
weapon, was He thinking about you and me? About our

ministries? About our marketing strategies?

In a way, I believe He was.

To get at Jesus's real meaning, I have to step back and get the big picture. Looking at His entire earthly ministry, I see Him operating with one over-arching priority: to connect the individual to his God. Anything that confused or interrupted that connection frustrated — even infuriated — Jesus. Here He was, far from home, plodding around in human skin, suffering the "slings and arrows of outrageous fortune," putting up with all manner of inconvenience (not to mention pain), and about to give His body to be battered and His life to be snuffed out — all for the sake of restoring the relationship between His Father and His children. And then to have someone complicate that, or forestall it, or obscure it — out of greed, out of pride, out of ignorance — must have been heartbreaking for Him.

This is what He found in the temple. In this facility, supposedly devoted to connecting people to God, profiteers were reducing the connection to an empty exercise of tradition. The sacrifices had been designed centuries earlier as an expression of people's contrition before God, and their devotion to Him — you reared your animals with care, you chose the best of the lot, you brought it to the temple and gave it over to God. But now the entrepreneurs had built up a fast-food version. You could go through the motions — offer God not a single thought until sacrifice day arrived — then show up at the temple and plunk down your money for a one-way ticket to forgiveness.

That's not *relationship*. That's a crass disregard of what the Father longs for ... an intimate intertwining of hearts between Himself and His creation!

Jesus didn't accidentally use the term *market* — or *marketplace* (in the New Revised Standard Version), or *house of merchandise*. The King James shows most clearly how He deliberately juxtaposes *my Father's house* with *house of merchandise*. Here He pinpoints the concept of *value exchange*. The people were called to exchange something of value from their lives (an animal) for something of value from God's life (forgiveness). It was a terribly lopsided deal, but God offered the exchange because of His outrageous love for people. Now, however, opportunistic self-seekers stepped into the middle of the exchange, having figured out a way to siphon off some value for themselves.

Those eager capitalists sitting outside the temple had made the same mistake that many, many Christian organizations make today.

They had come to think of ministry and marketing as separate things.

This is a mistake?

Yes. It is schizophrenia ... and in ministry, it's a Deadly Disease.

* * * * *

You may have heard this kind of phraseology in the offices of some Christian organizations:

"I have people who handle fundraising for me."

"They do our development; I just do ministry."

"We try to keep fundraising separate."

You may have even observed this concept in the structure of a ministry staff or the operations of the ministry. The ministry leader goes out and "does ministry." The marketing or development staffers stay inside and "do fundraising."

Keeping the two separate, on the face of it, doesn't seem dangerous — or even mistaken. In fact, it sounds honorable — sort of a ministry equivalent of the separation of church and state.

But separation of church and state wasn't God's idea. The state needs the influence of the church — civil government, after all, is ordained by God, and His design for government is fully compatible with His design for the church (according to Romans 13:1, 1 Peter 2:13, 14, and elsewhere).

Likewise, our marketing efforts need to be fully informed by our ministries. Their designs should be fully compatible.

> **℞** Ministry and marketing should <u>not</u> be separate — because treating ministry and marketing as separate entities carries with it enormous risks.

For one thing, the longer we make ministry and

marketing separate things, the more unlike each other they become.

By the time of that explosive scene in John 2, the salespeople outside the temple evidently had no great affection for the ministry going on inside, except as a source of profit. But it might not have always been so. Who's to say they didn't start out just like many modern-day ministry marketers: full of love for the ministry? They said to themselves, "Look at how these people love God! Look at how God moves in their lives as they devote themselves to Him in this way! How can I help them? How can more people participate? How can we help even city dwellers, who can't conveniently raise their own animals, to have a part in this wonderful process?"

Somehow, though, somewhere along the line, these "empowerers" of the ministry became more consumed by — more focused on — the empowerment process than on the ministry itself. Instead of ministering, in their own way, alongside the priests, they became exclusively "marketers." They could still cling to seemingly safe and accurate definitions — ministry connects people to God, and marketing *enables* that connection — but already you can see a comma dividing the two ideas. And that chasm grows.

There's a danger of drifting into an attitude that says this: Marketing is a carnal thing we do only because we have to in order to accomplish something spiritual. In other words, *We gotta keep selling these stupid doves, or a bunch of folks will never get into that wonderful temple.*

When we come to feel this way, we've moved into an even more serious stage of schizophrenia. Now one of our identities is "good," the other "bad." Now some of our staff do God's work, others do dirty work. Now our donors are not our friends and partners, but a necessary evil.

Do we really believe that a good spiritual harvest can be reaped if we are planting such bad seed in such a foul field?

This is not how God designed ministry to occur.

This is not how He dreamed of people becoming connected to Him.

God's idea is that the marketing — the communicating, the inspiring, the persuading — will grow directly out of the ministry itself.

Jesus told Nicodemus, "That which is born of the flesh is flesh; and that which is born of the Spirit is spirit" (John 3:6 KJV). It's been so since the beginning. On the sixth day of Creation, God decided that zebras would produce zebras and not centipedes (Genesis 1:24). We find the same truth in Job, in Isaiah, in 2 Corinthians, in Galatians: We reap what we sow.

> If my marketing is "fleshly," my ministry can't be "spiritual."

> A dishonorable request for financial help can't produce "neutral" dollars which somehow become "godly" when they flow into my ministry's work.

> This defies God's design!

It is not inherently dishonorable to ask someone

for help in your ministry. Paul asked, and did so boldly (and through direct mail!). Women's contributions helped keep Jesus' earthly ministry on the road; a ministry treasurer even had to be designated.

But to keep marketing as honorable as the ministry it strives to empower, the two must be inextricably intertwined. Marketing must be part and parcel of the ministry — and the opposite must *not* be true.

Furthermore, the marketing must be subsumed in the ministry ... not the other way around.

The marketing effort must reflect the character of the ministry. Marketing must operate on the basis of the ministry's values, not vice versa.

If this one-way flow is not observed, marketing instincts begin to influence ministry decisions ... and the ministry becomes simply an elaborate collection service.

What will our ministry do next month?

I dunno ... What will raise the most money?

Now the Holy Spirit no longer guides the work; He sits outside in the waiting room, while we consult our revenue reports. And the work He wants to accomplish — in the lives of those our ministry is helping, even in the lives of our donors themselves — goes undone.

On the other hand, when the flow of values is properly maintained, the character of the ministry is maintained, and the result can be genuinely God-pleasing. It's still, after all, His work.

How can we make sure that our ministry and our marketing are synonymous, and that we don't get the marketing cart before the ministry horse?

Ah (Hamlet would sigh), there's the rub.

* * * * *

Ministry/marketing schizophrenia — often an extremely subtle attitude, not expressed or even realized — manifests itself in a disheartening array of symptoms. Let's look at just three of the most frequently suffered.

> Can you identify any of
> these three symptoms in
> your ministry?

1. Detached Donor Syndrome

Review your communications with your donors: appeal letters, phone scripts, videos, the works. Do they reflect the concept of *"You* give me money so I can do ministry"? Look for phrases like "help us accomplish," "we need," "if you ... then we can," and so forth. Those are the ugly paw prints of schizophrenia.

Or do your donor communications express the idea, "Let's do ministry together"? Look for phrases like "you can accomplish," "you'll make," "you'll touch," "together, we will," and the like. This kind of language reflects the attitude that the donor is part of the team, that God is going to work through the entire ministry family to accomplish His plan.

2. Divided and Conquered Syndrome

Check your stomach. How do you feel when you arrive at work in the morning? Eager, relaxed, energized? Or tense, irritable, worried?

When a Christian organization sees its ministry and its marketing as separate things, that schizophrenia often grows into (or out of) an even more fractured environment. A ministry can become a virtual war zone, with board members maneuvering for position and power ... or the board and the ministry principal warily circling one another ... or the leader and executive staff regarding each other as adversaries ... or the staff holding the leadership up to secret scorn ... or the development agency and employees viewing each other as morons ....

Or any combination thereof.

Fractious staffs are tragically commonplace in Christian organizations. And turf warfare is a reliable sign of schizophrenia. In these ministries, not only have marketing and ministry come to be regarded as separate things, but each function of the ministry — each department, each office — has evolved into a miniature "state" all its own. In such Balkanized organizations, frustration runs high, efficiency runs low, and both the quantity and the quality of the ministry itself suffer grievously.

3. Absent Father Syndrome

In some organizations, the ministry principal only rarely participates in any meetings where marketing is being discussed. Sometimes the principal declines to attend marketing meetings, but has a manager report back to him for "sign-off" on what the marketing team has decided. Or he simply dictates from the isolation of his office what the marketing emphasis is to be — and the marketing team tries to make the best of it. Or (most dangerous of all) the principal stays out of it altogether, leaving an executive to make decisions on his behalf and a secretary to rubberstamp his signature onto appeal letters. In any event, the leader of the ministry stays above the marketing fray. This kind of situation often corresponds to mayhem in the ministry's marketing area (and in the ministry operation generally); in other cases, staff members way down the chain of command may set *de facto* ministry policy by acting as "gatekeepers" for the leader.

A friend who serves as a ministry marketing consultant described one organization where more than a dozen people passed judgment on every component of the marketing program before the leader ever saw it. In four years he never attended one marketing meeting; in fact, the marketing consultant never saw him face-to-face or carried on a phone conversation with him for the first three years. Consequently, the marketing program was "fed" up the line, with each staff and board member making his or her changes — until the final, pathetic, watered-down product was presented to the leader for his approval. No wonder the marketing consultant found himself in massive battles over "what the ministry is about" and "what the message ought to be"!

A ministry leader who separates himself from the marketing process does his ministry no service. He may have no God-given gift for marketing; he may have no instincts for marketing; he may be one of those leaders clearly raised up by God to accomplish a mission but also clearly unable to contribute ideas to the nuts-and-bolts of the ministry's marketing effort. And yet, he must be involved — because ministry is not like building Ford Tauruses. It is not assembly line work. It is the outgrowth of "community."

All three of these symptoms of schizophrenia — not to mention the many other symptoms, which could fill a book of their own — must be overwhelmed by the fresh realization that ministry is an expression of community. Dr. Gilbert Bilezekian of Willow Creek Community Church outside Chicago observes that community is the fundamental concept of the church because community is the fundamental concept of the Trinity. God exists in three Persons — has *always* existed in three Persons — and as the perfect expression of His multiple nature created *people*. Leaving Adam alone was "not good" (Genesis 2:18). He designed the church as an expression of community ("All the believers were together," according to Acts 2:44), not a mosaic of Lone Rangers. We are interdependent, like it or not, and learning to live and work together is the most basic task of the Church.

Accordingly, we must acknowledge the fact that ministry is a team sport. The principal is only one part of the team. The staff form other parts. Volunteers are a part of the team. A development agency may be part of your team. Perhaps most critical of all, *the donor is a part of the team*. We are all members of the body of Christ, and certainly your ministry is a significant, distinct component of that body. It follows, then, that your ministry must function by the same processes and within the same parameters as the body as a whole. And denigrating the role of any member of the body is ... well, a no-no.

No doubt you have read and heard 1 Corinthians 12:14-27 many times. But read it here again, with your fellow ministry workers and your donors in mind:

> Now the body is not made up of one part but of many ....
> If the ear should say, "Because I am not an eye, I do not belong to the body," it would not

for that reason cease to be part of the body.

If the whole body were an eye, where would the sense of hearing be? If the whole body were an ear, where would the sense of smell be?

But in fact God has arranged the parts in the body, every one of them, just as he wanted them to be.

("Arranged ... just as he wanted" means your donor is doing exactly what God called her to do. The marketing department is exactly where God determined they should be at this juncture. The leader of the ministry is ordained by God for exactly that role at exactly this time! Yikes! Can this be true?)

If they were all one part, where would the body be?

As it is, there are many parts, but one body.

The **eye** [read: *board of directors*] cannot say to the **hand** [read: *marketing department*], "I don't need you!" And the **head** [read: *ministry president*] cannot say to the **feet** [read: *donors*], "I don't need you!"

On the contrary, those parts of the body that seem to be weaker are indispensable ....

God has combined the members of the body and has given greater honor to the parts that lacked it, so that there should be no division in the body, but that its parts should have equal concern for each other.

If one part **suffers** [read: *marketing*], every part suffers with it; if one part is **honored** [read: *leader*], every part rejoices with it.

(Is this how your ministry operates?)

> Now you are the body of Christ, and each
> one of you is a part of it.

Ministry leaders have to ask themselves: Am I a member of the body of this ministry? Or do I see *myself alone* as the ministry?

Marketing staffers have to ask themselves: Do I see the donor as a member of the body of this ministry? Or simply as a target of my "discount dove sale" ... a tool to be employed in the process of accomplishing something else?

When we come to see our ministry as part of God's grand design, part of Christ's own body, we may find ourselves communicating differently with our donors — and with our colleagues on the job.

* * * * *

But there's another aspect to the Apostle Paul's teaching which applies — sometimes painfully — to our ministry marketing strategies.

It's the flip side of the "unity" concept.

> Each member of the body
> has a specialty.
>
> We are a community, yes, but
> a community of specialists.

You're an eye? You don't walk anywhere. You're a

foot? You can't see a thing. Everyone is united, but each devotes himself to his own calling — for maximum efficiency and ministry productivity.

This seems like a simple idea, but it can be tricky to live out in a ministry organization. High-level executives, for example, can get bogged down in the minutiae of semi-colons and italics, or devote themselves to that single complaint in a stack of ten thousand donor gifts. To laser-personalize, or not to laser-personalize? That is not supposed to be the executive's question.

This is most counter-productive at the top level. Ministry leaders need to focus heavily on donor relationships — that is, developing relationships with their donors. Perhaps some ministry leaders plunge deeply into the mechanics of their fundraising effort — particularly direct mail, where there are plenty of mechanics to plunge into — because they want to believe that the mechanical apparatus of their donor relations strategy *actually qualifies* as donor relations.

In other words, they are reluctant to get into a relationship with their donors — calling them, corresponding with them personally, meeting with them in groups or one-on-one — when this is the one marketing function that a ministry leader can do most effectively ... and which no underling can do quite as well. Not that every ministry head is a natural "people person" — many aren't. And there are plenty of good people who are not heads of ministries but are gifted at establishing and developing relationships with donors. But in far too many organizations the leader keeps his distance from his donors — letting that gifted employee or consultant do all that stuff alone. By not stretching beyond his comfort zone, by not "mixing it up" with his donors, the leader causes his ministry to fall shorter than it would in terms of donor involvement, response, and loyalty. Meanwhile, chances are he's meddling in areas that ought to be handled by a secretary, an editorial assistant, or a marketing specialist.

One other by-product of God's excellent "community-of-specialists" design is that each participant in the process is trusted to do his or her work — with minimal intervention or second-guessing by those with other specialties. Do you find that your marketing plan needs to be justified to your ministry leader's brother-in-law — or wife — or mother — or offspring — who has input on the subject strictly on the basis of the family tie? God may actually give marvelous insight and genuine gifts to members of a ministry leader's family ... but the family relationship itself bears no weight when it comes to the quality of an idea. The input of even the most gifted family members actually ought to be scrutinized with extra care, simply because of the likelihood that a relative will have undue automatic influence. This is never more true than in the area of marketing, where feelings tend to run strong — and yet certain hard sciences apply. At the risk of seeming harsh, one must acknowledge that the truth is the truth ... even if somebody's brother-in-law wishes it weren't.

> When one member of the body
> tries to do another's job,
> disaster's ahead.

> Try pedaling your bike with

your ears!

When a ministry worker at any level gets into an operation where he has no business, feelings can easily get hurt — and the ministry itself gets hurt.

This is more than just a
busted business principle.

It is a matter of contradicting
God's design.

When one member of the body
hurts another member of the
same body, we call it *masochism*.

At the very least, schizophrenia and masochism in a ministry organization — failure to work by the community-of-specialists model — dooms that organization to inefficiency. Employees duplicate each other's efforts. Some do what could be done — should be done — faster or better by others. Overworked workers don't get the essentials accomplished, or miss deadlines. Costs go up. Net return goes down. And the pressure inevitably goes up on your marketing effort.

Schizophrenia and masochism have a variety of side-effects, and ministries that suffer from these diseases concoct a number of responses to deal with them. There's a strong tendency to take aspirin for the symptoms, instead of doing the bloody work of transplanting the heart — getting a whole new attitude about how ministry happens. Ministry leaders struggle and scramble. They fire workers, hire others. Put a different person in charge of meetings. Design a form; make everybody fill it out. Et cetera, et cetera.

Many ministries take schizophrenia and masochism into the realm of accounting. They meticulously monitor each of their departments' expenditures and income. This is fine, on the face of it. But this often leads to a wrong-headed extreme: they want each component of the marketing strategy to return at least its own cost. Schizophrenia in full bloom: Each member must carry the same weight. Masochism fully ripened: You don't produce, I'll cut you off!

But this approach misses the fact that God's macro-design for our ministries also applies as a micro-design for our ministry functions. One friend is poor; his better-off friend helps him. One member is weak; the one who is strong props him up. The poor one has other gifts to give; even the weak one has a unique role to play in God's scheme of things. That's how the organism of the church is designed to function.

Likewise, in the stream of impressions you make upon your donor — the entire body of communications which together make up your marketing strategy — some components will have fundraising muscle; others will be lame. Yet the lame ones can be a blessing — to the donor, and ultimately, to the ministry.

A newsletter, for example, may cost a bundle, relatively, and return virtually nothing (although we've found ways to make newsletters profitable for ministries) — yet the information in that newsletter *feeds* the donor, deepens her sense of involvement, shows her how her investment is paying off, strengthens her loyalty to the

ministry. And the return on a future appeal letter package
— the muscle piece — is even stronger as a result.

> We must distinguish between
> <u>direct</u> response strategy
> and <u>information</u> <u>dissemination</u>
> strategy.

Direct response functions (phoning donors to ask for
money, sending them appeal letters) don't fare well as
conductors of detailed information. Many a ministry has
discovered this the hard way, as we shall see.

On the other hand, most information dissemination
devices (newsletters, books, brochures) don't stand alone
as effective collectors of contributions. We'll observe this,
too.

Yes, the flow of information and the sequence of
direct response devices coming into a donor's life from
your ministry should be *integrated*. Both streams should be
related to each other in content.

But no, the *results* of each and every item in both
halves of the strategy should *not* be the same — because
their purposes are not the same.

In fact, we encourage ministries to go *beyond* this
"some-functions-won't-make-money" view ... all the way to
a "some-functions-should-actually-*lose*-money" view.
Because donors are valuable members of the ministry
family, and their role is overwhelmingly one of giving
rather than receiving, we suggest that ministries

sometimes simply *give* donors something of value — no strings attached.

> Send a good book that will help the
> donor deepen her walk with Christ.

> Send a cassette tape with superb music.

> Send something that meant a lot to you,
> something you'd like to mean a lot to *her*.

Ministries taking this radical step find that the enthusiasm of their donors for the ministry dramatically deepens. Here the donor suddenly comes to realize that she is not simply a pawn on the chess board of your ministry's work; she is actually appreciated as a living, breathing *partner*, a human being who plays an important part in the ministry.

Does she react negatively because you've spent a little money to send her something thoughtful? Generally not, if your gift is modest and tasteful. Donors work hard; you need to take the risk of expressing your gratitude tangibly.

Sure, it will cost you something in the short run. Trust God to provide the financial need over the long haul.

* * * * *

One of the most profound and meaningful gifts you can give to a donor is the gift of prayer. Not the boilerplate promise of prayer tucked into the text of an appeal letter — but real, live prayer.

For years we have encouraged ministries to make arrangements to call their donors periodically for no other purpose than to inquire about their needs and pray with them and for them right then and there, on the phone.

This suggestion has been met with a considerable array of responses ... everything from "You've got to be kidding!" to "Why didn't we think of this before?"

Some ministries have grown out of certain religious traditions which do not emphasize personal, one-on-one, vocalized prayer; they are more oriented to silent prayer or corporate prayer. So we sympathize with the discomfort of some ministry personnel in the matter of praying for donors over the phone. But we have seen the enormous power of a personal phone call, with no appeal — just a word of encouragement and an offer to pray with the donor about their needs. It is the power to strengthen the faith of that donor.

And because we have seen donors' lives profoundly touched by such a gift, we are eager to see more ministries establish such a program.

Moreover, donors who have received such a call frequently embrace the ministry with more passion (this is why we call such a program "prayer bonding"), and this often has the happy side-effect of increasing their lifetime giving to the work.

(Even in the case of a ministry growing out of a religious tradition which does not emphasize personal, vocalized prayer, we would like to see an attempt at prayer bonding in which the caller only offers to pray for the donor's needs at some later time — perhaps even specifying the specific date and time at which prayer will be offered.)

The leaders of some ministries decline to engage in any prayer-related communication with donors because they want to avoid the appearance of "selling prayer." This is a valid concern. The offer to pray for a donor must be heartfelt and sincere. It cannot be a thinly veiled fundraising strategy. It has to be the function of a ministry dedicated to the spiritual health and life of the people who empower the work through their giving. (If the donor actually has the feeling that you're "selling prayer" — if even the honest, friendly offer to "pray for you" is interpreted as a marketing scheme — it may be that your donors see you only as a merchandiser. You may need a major realignment of your relationship with them.) One way to ensure pure motives: Commit to praying for your donors regardless of their giving record.

> Praying for your donors will do as much good for you as it will do for them — maybe more.

If we have a certain reluctance about prayer, we're exhibiting one of the most heartbreaking symptoms of schizophrenia. If we do not pray for our donors, we have seriously devalued some of the most crucial members of our team. (If we pray for our donors, but don't want them to tell us what their needs are, we're keeping our donors at arm's length, in a cool, business-style relationship.)

Prayer, after all, is the most fundamental activity in the life of any Christian. While many of us fall short — we don't talk to God often enough, maybe only when we have an emergency, and we *certainly* don't *listen* to God enough — prayer is still the ideal of our Christian walk. The flow of communication between ourselves and our God should become second nature over the span of our life in Christ.

Accordingly, our ministries should be born in prayer and nurtured in prayer.

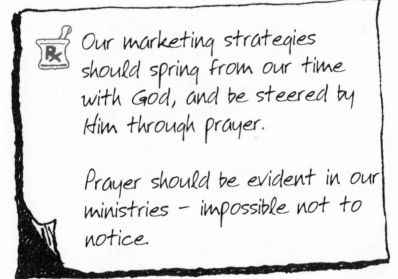

Our marketing strategies should spring from our time with God, and be steered by Him through prayer.

Prayer should be evident in our ministries — impossible not to notice.

Praying for our donors should be almost automatic, a "natural" outgrowth of who we are and what our ministries are.

When all the workers in a ministry are praying for

the ministry (and for each other, and for the donors), the Spirit of God has the chance to speak the same message to everyone, uniting the team and unifying the effort. Prayer, then, is the surest antidote for schizophrenia, for it allows a single Master to pull together all the specialists.

But be prepared: God is creative (He is the Creator, after all), and He may surprise you. We have seen more than one ministry turn an astonishing corner because God responded to fervent prayer — and radically reshaped the ministry.

Ronnie Metsker came to the helm of Kansas City Youth For Christ after his father's long and illustrious lifetime of service in that position. This dynamic youth-oriented ministry operates a number of outstanding facilities and programs designed to reach area teenagers with the life-transforming truth of the Gospel. But the ministry also owned a local television station — which siphoned enormous volumes of energy, time, and money from its youth-oriented ministry. Ronnie and his team prayed seriously about their situation — and clearly heard from God. They sold the station, in spite of significant public relations challenges, and turned their focus exclusively to teens. They have now embarked on a single, newly unified mission — and they are far more productive for it.

Paul S. Moore, the acclaimed "Shepherd of Times Square," launched Campus Crusade's urban-focus work (Here's Life Inner City), then established the unique CitiHope radio ministry, connecting the poor and homeless to listeners with the resources to help. But on a trip to Eastern Europe he was struck by the plight of the "children of Chernobyl" — and of the entire former Soviet republic of Belarus, which absorbed most of the radioactive poison spewing from the crippled power plant.

For some years, Paul pressed ahead with two ministries, the original CitiHope as well as a new CitiHope International, which took urgently needed medicines, food, and materiel to the hospitals and orphanages of Belarus. But the U.S. work floundered, and as he continued to pray about his ministries, Paul came to the profound realization that God had shifted his mission from America's cities to those of Eastern Europe. He folded CitiHope's ministry into that of Here's Life Inner City, under the extremely capable leadership of Ted Gandy — and Paul plunged heart and soul into Belarus. CitiHope International became one of the fastest growing charities in America; could this be evidence that God had a hand in the ministry's development?

It is often said that "prayer changes things." But in our human nature, we usually want the *other* guy to change. Change can be terribly uncomfortable.

But every living thing experiences growth and change.

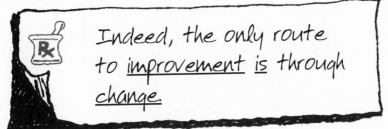

Indeed, the only route to <u>improvement</u> <u>is</u> through <u>change</u>.

Improvement, by its very nature,
is a change in the state of things.
To make your ministry more

effective is going to take
some changes.

Who better to suggest those changes than the
Creator of every living thing?

So we suggest talking with Him. Regularly. Say, at
least every day. Not just to ask Him for blessings on your
ministry. Ask Him to show you, continually, what part you
are to play in His ministry.

Make prayer a habit, an earmark of your life and
ministry. Move it up on your priority list. Pray for
direction, not just confirmation. See what God says about
your ministry. He may surprise you.

A pattern of prayer increases our chances for a
ministry "born of the Spirit" ... and decreases our chances
for a ministry "born of the flesh."

Which do you have?

Which do you want?

Chapter 3

DEADLY DISEASE #3: NEUROSIS AND CHARACTER DISORDER

I'm just like you, and I'm sick about it

M. Scott Peck, author of *The Road Less Traveled* and nobody's dummy, suggests that there are two kinds of people in the world.

You're either neurotic, or you're character disordered.

An inspiring view of mankind!

The terms are actually more frightening than the reality. Both refer to an individual's sense of responsibility. *Neurotic* simply speaks to the tendency of some people to assume more than their fair share of responsibility for any given dilemma. *Character disordered* refers to folks who assume *less* than their share. Neurotic people feel guilty. Character disordered people feel contempt for people who feel guilty.

Actually, Peck says, most people are at least a little of one and a lot of the other.

Only a few exceptionally healthy people are well balanced, with equal measures of neurosis and character disorder.

Already you're thinking, "Aunt Martha! That character disordered so-and-so!" or "That helpless, wimpy, neurotic husband of mine!"

Well, stop it. You're somewhere on the neurosis-vs.-character disorder scale yourself, y'know.

And your own guilt/contempt quotient influences your view of your donors ... influences your approach to ministry marketing ... influences your entire way of approaching ministry.

But wait! We can go Peck one better. For while he may be correct in saying that there are two kinds of people in the world, ministry marketing people aren't exactly regular people (are we?) — and we can see another type of distinction in their psyches.

> ℞ *Ministry marketers come in two varieties: those who look at their donors and say,*
>
> *"They're just like me,"*
>
> *and those who look at their donors and say,*
>
> *"They're not at all like me."*

I call these categories "identified" and "distinct." Of course, again, most of us aren't exclusively one or the other. But we tend to be strongly one or the other — probably more strongly than we realize. You're either highly identified with your donors, or you see yourself as highly distinct, quite different in perspective, from your donors.

Which complicates your neurosis or your character disorder considerably. You're somewhere on the neurosis/character disorder scale, and somewhere on the identified/distinct scale; and where the two intersect — well ... (Is this confusing? I'll draw you a chart in a moment.)

Let's say you're an identified neurotic. That means you figure the donor feels just like you do, and you think of the ministry as an intrusion into her life.

Or let's say you're distinct and character disordered. Then you think the donor isn't like you — she just needs to be told what to do — and she'll love it.

Or you can be identified and character disordered. Or distinct and neurotic.

Of this one thing you can be sure: you tend to be one of the four.

Why this long, involved psychology lesson?

Because your responsibility-and-identity profile strongly influences your view of ministry marketing — and your execution of your marketing strategy.

How will a neurotic marketer tend to communicate with his donors? Seldom. I *don't want to bother them.*

What tone will a character disordered marketer tend to take in communicating with his donors? Peremptory. *This is important; give!*

Where does the identified marketer look for ideas for communicating with his donors? Within. I *hate long letters; so does she.*

It is actually possible to map out the various responsibility-and-identity combinations on a grid, and pull together some of the most pronounced tendencies of the four "types" in their creation and execution of strategies for communicating with their donors. Boiled down to their simplest, most straightforward essentials, they look something like this:

	IDENTIFIED: (they're just like me)	DISTINCT: (they're not at all like me)
CHARACTER DISORDERED: (I'm not responsible)	They're one with me (they owe me) (I'll just tell them what I'm doing) short, peremptory informative letter	They're laypeople (they'll obey) (I'll just tell them to give) long, peremptory emotional letter
NEUROTIC: (I'm fully responsible)	They hate me (I'll be brief; infrequent) short, apologetic emotional letter	They know better (I'll inform them fully) long, apologetic informative letter

There's no question that these are generalizations. You can probably think of a number of individuals who seem to fit into one category or another, but who do not manifest their tendencies as indicated here. But these general descriptions more or less characterize people working in ministry development.

The important question is: Where on the grid do *you* live?

Do you feel a vague sense of embarrassment when it

comes to asking your donors for money? That's a symptom of neurosis — sorry!

Do you feel a certain level of anger welling up inside you when an appeal doesn't generate the donations you expected? That's your character disorder acting up again — oops!

We can look briefly at each of the four "inclinations" represented on the grid and discover *tendencies* that will probably emerge in the ministry marketing effort of the corresponding individual.

Identified, Character Disordered

This is the person who says to himself, "The donor is just like me — so much so, in fact, that I can just tell her what I'm doing, and she'll understand instantly and get on board." This person, then, tends to prefer short, staccato communications with his donors — one-page letters, emphasizing information over emotion. "I don't have to ring her bell," he tells himself, "because this ministry thrills her the same way it thrills me!"

This thinking often leads to the creation of donor communications with a "peremptory" tone — the tone that suggests the donor somehow "owes" the ministry a response. There's little or no effort to excite the donor's interest or imagination. Mail packages sent to donors tend to feel like basic collection devices.

Identified, Neurotic

This marketer sees the donor as himself, but worries about that. He assumes the ministry is intruding on the donor's life in an unpleasant way. So he tends to send very short communications to donors, and rarely. In some cases this type of marketer may tend to rely more on emotion than information — based on the feeling that "I don't want to bog the donor down with lots of data."

Distinct, Character Disordered

This is the marketer who tends to say to himself, "The donor isn't like me; the donor needs to be told what to do" — but who also fails to feel responsible for the care and keeping of the relationship with the donor. Such a view often results in donor communications which overwhelm the donor with passionate pleas for help — direct mail letters in this case tend to be longer and more emotional, with the feeling of "This is so important, you've just got to help me!" There's a sense of "you just don't understand" in these letters — an accidental talking "down" to the reader.

Distinct, Neurotic

Here's the marketer who feels that the donor must be enormously suspicious of the ministry, so he responds by overwhelming the donor with information. Letters tend to be long and jammed with detail, but not much emotion.

Each of these four types of marketing "personalities" has its own weaknesses — and thank goodness, most of us aren't extreme examples of any one of the four. But observing the natural inclinations of the four in their "pure" form may help us identify our own weaknesses.

Down through the years, we have found far more identified individuals than distinct individuals working in ministry development situations. In no fewer than one hundred separate marketing meetings, I have heard the following statement (with easily imagined variations): "If I get a letter like that, I throw it right in the garbage." Or: "I *hate* getting calls from telemarketers, and I know other people do, too." The urge to identify one's own likes and dislikes with the donor's likes and dislikes is overwhelming.

But it is rarely correct.

The identified position is most dangerous in a ministry leader. By definition, a leader is different from the average Joe or Joanne. The leader emerged into a position of leadership because he wasn't a follower.

If the donor were a leader like the leader is, then the donor would have her own ministry!

The identified ministry marketer feels that the donor's needs, motives, and priorities are essentially the same as his own — so he constructs donor communications as if he were talking to himself. So whether he writes long letters or short; emotional letters or straightforward; rational ones; pushy or apologetic; often or seldom — he still communicates in a way that fails to elicit much response from donors.

But it is possible for the distinct ministry marketer to arrive at the same undesirable result by a completely different route. By believing that the donor is unlike himself, the distinct marketer communicates in ways *opposite* to the approaches he would appreciate most himself. So, again — regardless of the length, frequency, or tone of his letters — he fails to get the maximum potential response from his donors.

What is happening here?

We can see the contrast between the ministry marketer and the ministry's donor (or prospective donor) in the story of the old man who was walking down the sidewalk when he heard a sultry female voice.

"Kiss me," the voice said, "and I'll make all your dreams come true."

The old man stopped walking and looked around for the source of the invitation. But he didn't see anyone, so he kept on walking. Then he heard it again:

"Come on, baby, give me a kiss and I'll make all your dreams come true."

The puzzled old man looked around again — and finally saw that the voice was coming from a frog sitting nearby.

"That's right, baby," the frog said. "I used to be a beautiful princess. Give me a kiss and I'll turn back into a princess — and I'll make all your dreams come true."

The old man silently picked up the frog, put it in his pocket, and kept walking.

"Hey!" the frog cried. "Why didn't you kiss me and let me make all your dreams come true?"

"I'm 83 years old," the man replied, "and at my age, I'm more interested in owning a talking frog."

The talking frog is a ministry like yours. The old man is a donor — like yours. And our job, as ministry marketers, is to get the old man to kiss the frog ... or rather, to motivate the donor to do something he might have some reluctance to do (give money), in order for the ministry to become something greater than it already is.

Why did the old man refuse the frog's tempting offer? Because it was only tempting from the perspective of the frog. The frog didn't think like the old man thought. The frog was thinking about her own needs. As a result, the frog didn't speak to the real needs of the old man, to learn about his motives and priorities.

Look at your account books. Why do so many donors decline to give to your ministry in any given month? Perhaps your requests for help seem compelling to you — but are uninteresting to the donor.

> The deadliest words ever spoken in a ministry marketing meeting are:
>
> "Here's something really interesting!"

Those of us who live in the rarefied atmosphere of ministry marketing, locked in a world of ministry employees, with nary a "civilian" to be found, come to be fascinated by our own ministry programs — but wrongly think of them as *fascinating* to donors. We are fascinated, not fascinating. Our donors have different needs, motives, and priorities than we do.

When you take a long, hard look at how many

donors *don't* respond to your requests for financial support, you may be forced to come to terms with the fact that you haven't made the difficult leap to thinking like a donor as you construct your appeals for support. Perhaps you don't have a handle on your donors' real needs, motives, and priorities.

When I teach ministry marketing personnel, I insist on using the crass terms *buyer* and *seller* rather than *donor* and *ministry*. I do this in hopes of exploding ministry marketers out of their cozy, comfortable world, wherein they're doing the Lord's work and everybody loves them for it. The hard truth is that when the ministry is contacting a donor or prospect and asking for a financial gift in response, the ministry is *selling* a proposition. The donor, regardless of how noble her heart, is *buying* the proposition. There is absolutely an *exchange of value*, just like at your local grocery store, as the ministry offers something (even if it's only the joy of knowing you're making a difference) and the donor agrees to give something in return for it.

My friend in ministry Tom Schermitzler wisely observes that buying and selling are imperfect metaphors.

"I did not choose to be in ministry, like a grocer chooses to sell food," he points out. "Instead, I was 'called' to be in ministry. So it is God's responsibility to connect me with the right people. I am responsible to serve — not sell — the ministry."

All of which is true ... except that there's more.

"Even if I see myself as a steward and not a seller," Tom adds, "I still need to represent the ministry in the best way — a way that is easily accessible and appealing to those I am ministering to. This requires 'marketing.'"

There is nothing shameful in this process. Even the Apostle Paul, in his "thank-you letter" to the Philippians, noted the precise value exchange which occurs when individuals support ministry:

> "Not that I am looking for a gift,
> but I am looking for what may
> be *credited to your account*"
> (Philippians 4:17).

God calls on us to give to ministry (Luke 10:7 and elsewhere), and He promises blessings accordingly (Luke 6:38 and elsewhere). Maybe God doesn't call many millionaires to set up independently wealthy ministries because it would rob so many people of the blessings that come from giving!

In any case, when the ministry expresses its need to the donor, the selling-and-buying phenomenon occurs. The seller presents the case for buying, and the buyer judges the merits of the case. In thousands of ministries, the seller thinks and talks and acts like the seller — when in fact, the buyer is a very different kind of creature.

We see this phenomenon in the marketing of products, services, and events. The owner of the big stadium is biting his nails over the upcoming Mack & the Knives concert. Will he lose money for lack of ticket-buyers? He writes a spot and puts it on the radio: "Plenty of good seats available!" he proclaims. He is thinking like a seller: he's got loads of seats to fill, and he thinks of them as *good*. But I'm driving along in my Buick and I hear his radio spot. Mack & the Knives? I may have heard of them; I might be interested. Then I hear the magic words:

"Plenty of good seats available!" What does this say to me, in my role as the buyer? *Nobody's going. This concert is a dog.* The stadium owner has driven me away by thinking, talking, *smelling* like a seller — instead of like me, the buyer.

This phenomenon is so common in marketing that we have a code name for it: POGSA — which stands for (surprise, surprise) "Plenty Of Good Seats Available." Whenever I find myself writing a ministry marketing package which sells from the ministry's point of view instead of the donor's point of view, I've got POGSA on my hands ... and it's time for a rewrite.

Do you want to think about your donor reading your appeal letter over her garbage can, deciding within the space of about eight seconds whether to throw it away or not? She probably is. Horrified? Of course you are. You're the seller. She's not.

Do you like to think about your donor impatiently glancing through the contents of your direct mail package, barely reading any of it, before deciding if she'll respond? She probably does. She's a buyer. She's not you.

Do you enjoy the idea that she may start reading your letter and come across something she doesn't quite understand — and just *give up*, dumping your whole appeal for no better reason than *that*? It happens. That's what buyers do. And sellers *hate* it when that happens.

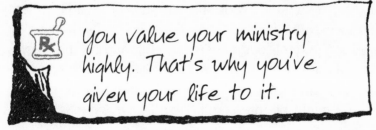

You value your ministry highly. That's why you've given your life to it.

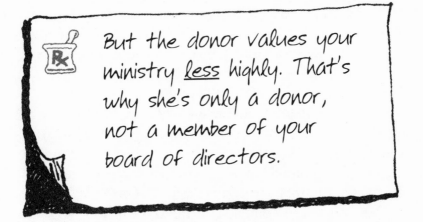

But the donor values your ministry _less_ highly. That's why she's only a donor, not a member of your board of directors.

Do you want to understand your donor, so you can communicate effectively with her?

Here's what we've found out about donors after years and years of studying them:

She is far more typical of _all_ donors to Christian ministries than you want to believe.

When we define the typical donor, the hair stands up on the necks of many ministry marketers. "Our donors aren't like that." "Our donors are younger — more educated — less emotional" — whatever.

But then we run a test, a survey, or a study — and we find that the donor file is by and large _very similar_ to the average Christian ministry donor file in many important ways.

Of course each ministry cultivates a family of donors unique to itself in key ways — an India evangelism ministry cultivates donors interested in India evangelism, for example — but these are not major distinctives which affect marketing *strategy*.

She's a "she."

The overwhelming majority of donors to Christian organizations are female. They are mothers, grandmothers, and widows. They are single and married. Even when a donor appears in your records as "Mr. and Mrs. Douglas Brendel," chances are that Mrs. Brendel is opening your letters and writing your checks.

Yet how many women sit at the table in your ministry's marketing meetings? Probably a minority.

A few generations ago, ministry might have been conducted effectively according to the sexist stereotype, with men dictating strategies in order to impact an audience of men. But no more. The buyers are women, and the sellers need to learn to think like women.

She is probably older than you would prefer.

We want to believe our ministries are attracting young donors who will carry our work into the future. If we're baby boomers, we tend to think of our donors as vital young Eisenhower babies like ourselves! (In a bizarre episode, we actually lost a client simply by revealing to the ministry principal the truth about the age of the ministry's donors. We ran a demographic study, the donors turned up every bit as elderly as we had predicted, and the ministry leaders fired us — a classic case of "shoot the messenger"!)

But the truth is, older donors tend to have more

income which they consider disposable, and they tend to be freer to give.

The brilliant Christian fundraiser Dan Scalf observes that many older donors have lived during very tough times, which leads them both to appreciate what God has given them and to relate more easily to the need of others. "They are also reaching the point in their life," Dan says, "where they begin to look back over the years gone by and ask, 'What have I done with my life that is worthwhile?' That makes a significant impact on their giving decisions."

Yes, a few ministries have deliberately pursued younger donors, but in the great majority of cases we have found ministry marketing personnel to be surprised by the relatively advanced age of their donors.

Our propositions, then, need to be presented in ways that appeal to women who were born in 1945 or *earlier*. An appeal letter package written and designed with the values and suppositions of the 1940's and 50's in mind is a very different package from one that springs from the 1990's.

If you want to cultivate younger donors, you will probably have to segregate them into a separate file — or sacrifice some (maybe many) older donors who are providing a major portion of the ministry's revenues. (The age of your donors should particularly affect the size of type you use when you present your need in print!) In fact, it is extremely difficult to make the case for cultivating younger donors simply because of the enormous financial risks involved. As Dan Scalf has wisely warned, "even attempting to cultivate younger donors will be deadly for most who attempt it." He observes only two ways to get younger donors to give consistently:

(1) Get them physically involved in the work.

(2) Attach their giving to self-help resources.

So — it may be the better part of wisdom for your ministry to continue cultivating donors who are moving into the middle-aged category.

She is busy.

We want to think that our donor will drop everything when our letter or phone call arrives at her house. But as James Carville understood (see Deadly Disease #1), the buyer is living her own life. The seller has to make himself a *welcome interruption*.

This is one big reason why ministry marketers absolutely must give enormous attention to the "teaser" — the text which appears on the outer envelope of a mailing — or the initial seconds of a phone call to a donor. The donor isn't a donor at that moment; she's just a woman with a funny sound coming from her washing machine who's wracking her brain to remember what she did with that recipe her husband liked. The teaser has to cut through all manner of mayhem to get through to her!

She is bored.

Well, at least relatively speaking. The buyer is not automatically fascinated by what you have to sell. Only your very few, very most passionate, loyal donors are as passionate as you about your ministry. The typical Christian donor, in fact, is a donor to a number of Christian organizations. She is not only relatively *casual* about your cause, she is also (horror of horrors) interested in _other_ causes! The buyer must be regarded as having no significant incentive to take time with your appeal, to process it, to respond to it.

This is why every donor communication must be constructed from the buyer's viewpoint. Every letter must be about _her_, not about you.

She is a bad reader.

The typical donor doesn't read as well as you, because the typical adult doesn't read at a level as high as the typical manager or executive — and ministry marketers are managers and executives. So long, complicated words and sentences won't help you much in stating your case; in fact, they could hurt you.

We find that the visual construction of a direct mail package must suggest to the busy, bored, bad reader that she can absorb the message of the package in only a few moments. That's why we recommend lots of short paragraphs, bite-size morsels, floating in lots of white space. If she glances at a letter and sees paragraphs of six lines or more, she receives a mental "alert": _Danger! Danger! This will take too much time and energy to absorb!_

We also like to give this bad reader a few helps to draw her impatient eye through the appeal: underlining, margin notes, and the occasional paragraph stacked on a narrow column all help her to hop, skip, and jump through the letter with minimal effort.

The goal is for the buyer to be done absorbing the message of the appeal before she even realizes what has happened!

But now bundle up all these sad things we can learn about the donor (she's older, distracted, not much interested in us, and a bad reader) — and all these disturbing things we can learn about ourselves (we're neurotic or character-disordered, distinct or identified) — and where does it leave us? On the therapist's couch? No — we've just come to terms with *reality*, and that's where you get out of *therapy*.

But this still doesn't solve our ministry marketing problem. It can help to know the donor intimately, and it can help to know ourselves intimately, but it's not the whole solution to the donor-response puzzle. We can have all this information and still fail to get a response from the donor.

How?

Because we still haven't established a *relationship* with the donor.

Chapter 4

DEADLY DISEASE #4: LEPROSY

Love me — now go away

I visited Tala, the largest leper colony in the Philippines — a country where they still *have* leper colonies.

Tala is an entire city, with a population of 10,000.

It has its own mayor, its own city hall, its own police and fire department.

There's a hospital, a school.

The only difference between Tala and any other town of its size in the Philippines is that all the people there are lepers.

Leprosy victims move there, then their spouses and children move there because they miss them so much.

Because leprosy is transmitted by prolonged physical contact, the spouses and children get leprosy too.

And when babies are born into Tala's families, they inevitably contract the disease as well.

It is a city founded, ironically, on shattered relationships. Actually, leprosy can usually be transmitted only by prolonged intimate physical contact — yet it has such a horrible reputation that a leper is outcast in normal social circles. He can't work, can't interact. Society literally cuts him off. Hence, leper colonies.

Unfortunately, this brutal imagery fits many ministries quite accurately.

They cut off their donors — shut down channels of

communication — isolate donors outside the circle of their ministry.

I found the people of Tala to be warm, wonderful, loving, giving people ... but Filipino society at large never benefits from the contributions these citizens could make. Likewise, in our ministries, donors and potential donors fade into the distance, and our ministries don't realize the benefit of their contributions.

The only difference between Tala and our ministries is that the Filipinos deliberately isolate their lepers. We do it by accident.

We fail to establish and cultivate *relationships*.

It comes as a surprise to many ministry personnel that the ideal means of generating response from a donor is to establish a relationship with that donor. The phrase *relationship marketing* has been so overused and abused in recent years that it's no wonder many avoid it. Some hear *relationship marketing* and think "warm, fuzzy letters that don't really ask people for help." Some ministries have gone down this muddy road only to find their revenues sunk up to the axles.

But let's abandon such a definition of relationship marketing. Let's look at relationship for what it really is: an essential component of any response.

How, after all, does response occur? Let's look at the process backwards, to see where the donor's response came from:

The buyer buys.
That's **RESPONSE**.

What did it take for the buyer to buy?

It took **CONVICTION.**
It took being *convinced* that the proposition was worth
responding to.

By what process did the buyer come to such a conviction?
It was the process of **PERSUASION.**
The seller brought the buyer along, at a certain pace, to a
place of *confidence* in the decision she was about to make.

By what means did that process of persuasion take place?
It took place by way of **COMMUNICATION.**
Persuasion can't happen in a void. It requires a
transmission of information.

But if I'm busy, bored, or a bad reader, I can cut off the
communication at any moment.
The housewife can close the door on the vacuum
salesman whenever she wants.
*How did it happen that the buyer allowed the communication
to continue?*
Answer: There was **RELATIONSHIP.**

The seller got the buyer's attention. The seller cut
through the mayhem of the day by *relating* to the buyer —
talking to her about something in the realm of *her own
needs, motives, and priorities.* This initial expression of *relating*
elicited an instant, instinctive response of interest from
the buyer — a bit of visceral feedback.

The seller went on, transmitting more information,
continuing to relate to the buyer's situation, and weaving
in the seller's proposition. The buyer continued to
respond with attention.

If the two had been carrying on a face-to-face conversation, the buyer would have offered positive responses: "Mm-hm," "Yes, I see," and nods of the head. But that's not possible in a letter-writing and -reading situation, the means by which many ministries solicit the lion's share of their contributions. All we can hope for is that the buyer will continue to allow the information to be transmitted. In other words, we hope she'll keep reading.

We know she won't keep reading if she senses no reason to. She has to relate somehow to what is being shared. This is the basic, clinical definition of *relationship*. But the warm, human concept of relationship is what enables basic, clinical relationship to occur!

> If I'm reading a letter that engages me — that connects to the deep-down-inside-of-me person that I perceive myself to be — I'll enter into a relationship, if only for a few moments, and allow myself to consider responding.

But if what I'm reading doesn't feel like a valuable relationship, I'll bail out.

Think back to that frog soliciting a kiss from the old

man. How much further might the frog have gotten if she had been able to involve the old man in a relationship?

Innumerable ministry organizations haven't involved their donors in a personal relationship. Which is doubly sad — not only because the ministry benefits enormously from the increased response of donors in relationship, but also because relationship with a donor isn't as difficult to accomplish as it may seem.

> **℞** The components of a successful donor relationship are very much the same as the components of a successful friendship.

You talk to your friends in a certain way. You reveal certain things to your friends. You lower your guard with your friends in ways that you don't lower your guard with, say, the Fed Ex courier. And fortunately, in the case of most ministry organizations, much of your relationship with your donors is conducted through the mail, which is a very private venue for communicating the private thoughts that only friends would exchange.

This, then, is the heart of donor response.

Look at the ways friends communicate, and you'll find the best way to establish relationship with your donors. (Some call it "friend raising," not fundraising!)

Does this seem simple-minded — to study

"friendship" as a means of building a ministry organization's revenues? We've found in working with dozens of ministries that it's completely appropriate. If we see our donors as members of our ministry family, it only follows that a friendly relationship should deepen our involvement with each other. (Sadly, many ministries think they have friends or "partners" when the organization really hasn't done anything to cultivate the relationship.)

Down through the years, I've frequently taught the components of friendship and applied them to ministry marketing. These components of friendship have come directly out of the settings in which I've taught. In almost every session I have asked attenders to call out the reasons why their best friend is their best friend, and I write these reasons on a board or overhead transparency. We have yet to find any serious foundations of actual "best friendships" which do not fall into one of these categories. The specific terminology may be different, but the meanings are consistent.

The idea of friendship as a basis for communication is not unique to ministry marketing. I have been called on to teach the same concepts to seminary students as they learn to preach and teach. How often have you heard a sermon which seemed to bear no relation to you or your current circumstances? While God promises that His Word will not "return void" (Isaiah 55:11), that sermon could certainly have made more of an impact on your life — probably on a number of lives — if it had been constructed more thoughtfully as an expression of true *relationship* between the preacher, the Word, and you. Pulpit ministers who learn to suffuse their teaching with the components of friendship generate a far greater level of response; that is, more members of their congregations make decisions to change their views and behaviors based on the principles of Scripture which the minister has expressed.

Okay, okay — so what *are* the components of friendship? Let's take a look … No, wait. First, a disclaimer: Some of the categories overlap. Oh well, life is inexact. In any event, the more your communications with your donors reflect these various components, the better able you will be to relate to your donor — the better able your donor will be to relate to *you* — and the greater the level of your donor's response to your appeals for support.

One more note: no single component of friendship reflects the sum total of a relationship. Some friendships thrive with only a few of the components, but no true friendships grow out of just one or two. You may have a friendly *acquaintance* with someone on the basis of a handful of these components, but probably no deep and abiding friendships.

In the next ten minutes, we'll discover nine ways in which it happens — or doesn't.

How many of the nine are true of your interaction with your donors?

Chapter 5

WILL YOU BE MY FRIEND?

The stuff of friendship is the stuff of donor relations

Friendship works just like your relationships with your donors work. Make yourself a checklist. As you ride the friendship rollercoaster for the next few minutes, ask yourself how many of the following traits of friendship mirror your communications with the people who support your ministry. The answer may surprise you ....

1. Commonality

Certain things are true of everyone. All human beings — certainly most adults in our Western culture — share certain experiences. Donor communications should refer to common, everyday occurrences. It's only logical: the fewer everyday experiences two people share in common, the less likely they are to form a deep and abiding friendship.

The ministry principal signing the letter needs to become, in the donor's mind, a regular everyday person. "I was stuck in traffic the other day, and ..." You share certain human interests and concerns with your donors, simply because you're both people. Talk to your donor about your family, or your car breaking down, or your dog dying, and you'll have the donor's interest — because you're on *common ground* with her.

Many ministry marketers make the mistake of discussing only "ministry business." This suggests that the only thing the donor has in common with you is the work of the ministry — an extremely narrow bridge over which to build a relationship. Sure, someone who has given to your ministry shares certain interests and concerns with you. But this doesn't mean the donor is as deeply interested or as deeply concerned about these ideas as you are, just that you're on the same basic track. If I recognize a number of ways in which you and I have things in common, I have many more opportunities — and many more reasons — to continue allowing communication from you. In this way, our relationship advances.

Jesus is well-known as an ideal example of commonality in communication. He used the everyday scenes of the culture of His day as the backdrop for His teachings. His parables were about cleaning women and farmers and bothersome neighbors. He surely could have used more complicated or technical language — but He had a higher priority than impressing His audience with fancy language. He wanted to *connect*. So He used plain, ordinary words. So should we.

2. Information

This seems extremely rudimentary, but it's an essential component often missed in communications with donors. Friends share information.

Some ministries attempt to generate funds virtually on the basis of emotion alone.

"This is exciting!" they say.

"I'm so excited about this!" they say.

"This is a tremendous opportunity!" they say.

Maybe so. But this can't be the substance of the

case you're making. Emotion is crucial to the request for help (as we shall see), but it must be balanced with information. You must share the facts of the situation with which you want the donor to become involved.

For years we helped in the raising of funds for a local Chicago-area ministry. Both Dale Berkey and I used to live in Chicago, but working now from our offices in Ohio and Arizona, we found ourselves creating direct mail packages which the client considered "generic." The client felt that our letters could be used by any similar type of ministry in any city. The client was right. We were bringing too little *information* to the packages — information unique to that ministry and to those donors. So we began receiving the Sunday *Chicago Tribune* each week, in hopes of bringing a fresher supply of unique-to-Chicago information into the appeals.

Even more important than using information about the locale, however, is the challenge of bringing information about the ministry — what it is doing, how and where and when and why and with whom.

> ℞ The fuzzier you are in communicating the facts about <u>what</u> <u>will</u> <u>be</u> <u>accomplished</u> with the money the donor sends you, the leerier the donor will be about sending you money in the first place.

Jesus demonstrates the importance of information transmission. Read straight through the Sermon on the Mount (Matthew 5-7) and you get the queasy feeling of "information overload."

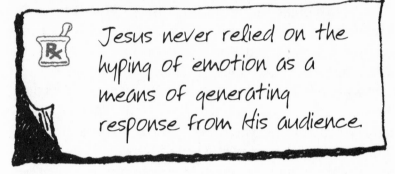

Jesus never relied on the hyping of emotion as a means of generating response from His audience.

He laid out His case clearly — He stated facts (we like to call them *truths*) — but in a way that kept His listeners engaged.

As a result, Christianity does not require us to check our brains at the door. It is a thinking person's faith. It is rational and comprehensible. Yes, it's thrilling — but the emotion we feel is based on fact. Jesus transmitted actual information. So should we.

3. Colloquialism

Colloquialism is just a big fancy word for *not using big fancy words*. Forget about perfect college-paper composition when you're writing a letter to your donors.

Write from your heart.

Save the King's English for your highbrow journal articles and books if you want to, but when you send a letter, type it on a plain typewriter, write a P.S. by hand, say what you really mean, and say it how you feel it.

If your organization employs an editor who keeps formalizing your letters for the sake of your public image, fire the editor and open your heart to your donors. They're your friends.

Speaking plain English is more of a problem in ministries today than you might imagine. Many ministry principals want to be regarded as sophisticated; others surround themselves with staffers who want the principal to be regarded as sophisticated. Some ministry leaders and workers simply make the common error of switching to formal English whenever they move from the spoken word to the written. An individual who can carry on a warm face-to-face conversation with you suddenly turns into William F. Buckley when he writes you a letter.

In the scriptural record, Jesus never wrote anything down — never turned anything into a formal business letter. His message was communicated strictly by word of mouth — and He spoke Aramaic, the plain-English equivalent of His day. He "put the cookies on the bottom shelf," easily accessible to the common people. So should we.

There is a ministry leader who appears on television — one of the most powerful and effective heart-to-heart communicators we've ever seen. He speaks plain English on his programs — some might even call it "down home" — and we see incredible results through his ministry. God uses this man's unique communication gifts to effect dramatic transformations in people's lives. But when his staff receive a proposed fundraising letter from the ministry's agency, they descend on the text like editorial ants, re-fabricating perfectly understandable phrases into medical-journal terminology, graying down colorful phrases, reconstructing common contractions ("I can't" becomes "I cannot"), and peppering the sentences with semi-colons. They see themselves as doing the man a favor — when in fact they are digging a great chasm between him and the people who have responded so warmly to him via television.

It is also wise to go *beyond* common English, turning an appeal letter into a virtual transcription of the spoken word. This doesn't make the letter look like a formal business communication, but it's a worthwhile sacrifice, because it has the effect of *connecting* to the reader. When a ministry comes to us for development help, we regularly give them a full page of disclaimers about the direct mail packages we'll be preparing for them — because inevitably, a former English major on the ministry staff reacts with horror to our proposed mailings. Here, in part, is what it says:

Do You Wonder?
Why Direct Mail Breaks the Rules
True Confessions from Berkey Brendel Sheline

Because letter-style direct-response packages designed for development or fundraising purposes must meet *response* standards — which is a fancy way of saying This Letter Must Raise Money — these standards sometimes override traditional punctuation and grammatical principles.

For example: We are always very concerned in direct response about carrying the reader's eye forward from phrase to phrase, from thought to thought, because of the average reader's strong inclination to "scan" fundraising packages rather than read them carefully.

Consequently, we subscribe to quite a complex science of alternative punctuation, unorthodox capitalization, and sentence fragmentation — all of which increases response to a package, but sometimes drives secretaries and editors batty!

For example, we make significant use of ellipses (...) and dashes (—), and frequently use capital letters after these items, even though a capital is not technically called for.

This has the surprisingly strong effect of holding the reader's eye — and generally does not reflect too negatively on your reputation for editorial precision, since most readers don't process their mail through a mental filter of "the rules."

This "science" of direct response also accounts for short paragraphs, increased use of commas, indented paragraphs, centered or otherwise realigned text, mid-sentence page breaks, use of hyphens where they might otherwise be omitted (like *re-aligned* instead of *realigned*), starting sentences with bridge words like And, Or, But, an ellipsis or dash —

and a number of other oddities.

So, then, please bear with us — as we break up paragraphs into bite-sizes with ellipses ... and dashes — and <u>underlining</u>

and odd margins

and Strange Caps and sentence fragments and even perhaps the occasional ALL CAPS OUTBURST!

Also — to help you get more out of the creative materials we've prepared for you:

• Letter-style packages should be produced to look like letters. Type, don't typeset. Do not justify the right margin; too stuffy.

• **Use 10-pitch type (10 characters per inch), preferably Courier, as we have done. Elite or 12-pitch type (12 characters per inch) is 20% less readable — and this will cut down on response.**

Rest assured that we are constructing your letter package with great care and precision, for the sake of maximum response, even if we don't always observe traditional punctuation and grammar.

Don't hesitate to feed back to us if you find there's something here you can't live with. In the meantime, it's an honor to serve alongside you in your ongoing work!

4. Truthfulness

"Oh, for heaven's sake," I hear you muttering. "Of course we're going to be truthful!"

Certainly. Friends don't lie to each other. True friends don't shade the truth. But in our communications to donors, are we really willing to lay it on the line?

"We need $12,000 by March 15th."

We couldn't admit that.

Why not? It's the truth. Say what you need. Say why. Say what will happen next.

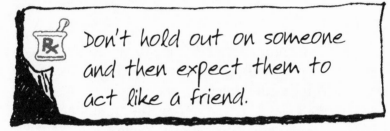

Down through the years we have often witnessed this scenario: the ministry leader refuses to tell his donors the truth about the ministry's need; then he gets to the point of having no choice, and the donors say, "Why didn't you tell us sooner! We would have helped you avoid this situation!"

Of course, by the same token, you can only cry wolf when the wolf is at the door — not before — or you'll trash your donor friendships.

Truthfulness has a marvelous way of smoothing otherwise troubled waters. For example: if you have to lean hard on your donors, acknowledge that you're leaning hard. "I know I've asked you to help me with this just as recently as three weeks ago, but ..." This is truthful. It acknowledges that you have a need, but it acknowledges how the donor might feel about being asked. It is deadly to over-apologize — but essential to acknowledge an unusual situation. You realize that donors are friends, not matchsticks to be struck, used, and tossed smoking into the ashtray. Think about how they'll feel when they read your letter — then accommodate those feelings as you talk to them.

Jesus did not restrict His truth-telling to the fun stuff. He expressed the hard truth along with the easy. So should we.

5. Consistency

You can count on your friends to be a certain way, to have a certain outlook, to perform at a certain level. There's a certain consistency to their character, to their goals, to their way of doing things. They're not always blindsiding you with a radical new "them."

In the same way, as you communicate with your donors, be yourself. Be the same person all the time.

One common scenario in ministry marketing is the bored ministry marketer.

We grow tired of stating and restating our mission.

We imagine the donor must be tired of it too.

So we switch gears — sometimes too radically.

What we've forgotten is that the donor's life is that raging river, and each impression we make is like throwing in that little pebble: the ripples disappear almost instantly. Our message is much fresher to the donor than to us, after we've soaked in it day-in and day-out, month after month!

My friend the late Ben Brannock, a great fundraising writer who worked for a variety of nonprofit organizations as well as Jack Kemp's 1988 presidential campaign, took this concept to an amazing extreme. Ben claimed that the vast majority of donors are so busy, so casual, and such bad readers that you could take a well designed letter package and mail it to a charity's mailing list *once a month for an entire year*, absolutely without alteration and absolutely without explanation, and the package would generate *more income* over time rather than less. Ben said that in response to the sequence of mailings, the typical donor would talk to herself more or less as follows:

"Hm." (Tosses package in garbage.)

"Hmm." (Tosses package in garbage.)

"Hmm, what's this?" (Opens envelope, looks at lead paragraph, tosses package in garbage.)

"Hmm, what's this?" (Opens envelope, looks at lead paragraph, glances at other components in package.) "Hmm." (Tosses package in garbage.)

"Hey, I remember hearing something about this." (Opens envelope, glances through package, tosses package in garbage.)

"Hey, I've been hearing good things about this." (Glances through package, thinks about it a second — doorbell rings — tosses package in garbage.)

"Hey, this is a really good idea." (Glances through package, sets reply card and envelope on stack of bills to pay, later loses reply envelope, tosses reply card in garbage.)

"Hey, I've been wanting to get involved with this kind of thing for a long time." (Sets reply materials on stack of bills, writes check later, along with utilities payment.)

Would Ben's idea work? Can't say. Sadly, none of Ben's clients would ever let him test his theory. But the concept behind his idea is valid. Working in the ministry, looking from the inside out, we tend to perceive the ministry's communications far more intensely than our donors, who are looking at the ministry from the outside in — and even then, only *glancing*. As ministry marketers, we get our fill. "We've told our donors already; how can they stand to be told again?" Tell them again anyway.

> ℞ Your donors are not nearly as full of your message as you are – and not nearly as full of your message as you need them to be!
>
> What is your ministry about? Tell them again. Then tell them again.

> Beat the drum of your mission statement, and beat it relentlessly.

A ministry must hew to its mission — resisting not only its own marketers' boredom but also the urge to do and say things simply for the sake of getting a response.

I have a dear friend in ministry who learned this lesson the hard way. Let's call him Dave, since that's not his name. Over the course of many years, Dave was about one thing. He made that clear to his donors, and they supported him in it. When he communicated, he was informative, entertaining, spoke plain English, you get the idea. But a friend of Dave's, another minister, was having better success at fundraising through the mail. This friend was about something completely different. Dave got the idea that he could raise more money for his own thing by *becoming like his friend* in his direct mail communications with his donors.

Did it work? No. His donors fled. Dave wasn't himself anymore. He wasn't about what *they* were about — the mission that he had inspired them to become a part of.

By the time he corrected his course and turned back to his original persona, Dave had lost lots of his old friends — and the new friends he had acquired were conditioned to expect the *new* Dave.

Dave could never be just one thing again ... and his ministry never fully recovered.

To translate the concept of consistency into the *look* of our communications with donors is a constant challenge. Dave, as one sad example, had always done interesting-looking mailing packages — but always within a certain framework of good taste. His outer envelopes featured intriguing teasers; his letters were lively and entertaining, well-balanced between information and emotion. We always knew where our money was going when we sent it to Dave. But when he switched gears and tried to become more like his friend, Dave began mailing wildly inconsistent mail packages: outer envelopes covered with badly cut-out photographs, screaming tabloid-style headlines, wild variations in typefaces and styles, you name it. The only way Dave might have gotten away with such mailings would have been to mail that kind of stuff from the beginning of his ministry!

The opposite problem, of course, is the commitment to identical dull packages for mailing after mailing. Repetition in and of itself isn't necessarily wrong; but the repetition of a boring presentation tends to decrease response. Ministry personnel have offered us an impressive array of excuses for hewing to such an approach:

"It gives us a strong, corporate feel."

"We cut costs by buying envelopes in bulk."

"We don't have the personnel to create a unique look every time."

"We don't want to look like tacky fundraisers."

Unfortunately, identical corporate-looking mail packages often have the unpleasant side-effect of *lower response rates* because more people tend to respond more warmly to a personal appeal than to a corporate one.

What you save in discounted bulk envelope printing, you more than lose in flattened response to the appeals they carry; what you save in salaries or fees for creative packaging personnel, you more than lose in flattened response to the vanilla packages you send without them!

And creative package design doesn't automatically equate to a "tacky fundraiser" look; there are plenty of dignified, classy, yet interesting approaches to direct mail design that can maintain your integrity while still engaging the recipient's interest.

> ℞ Neither a wacko, off-the-wall, never-know-what-to-expect approach nor a dull, plain, monotonous approach will generate maximum relationship with, or response from, your donors.

Jesus' earthly ministry was fully integrated. He expressed Himself through a dazzling array of techniques and revealed a wide variety of emotions — but we can look over the whole of His life and teachings and see His single over-arching mission of reconciling people to God. Jesus did not get sidetracked on Satan's political campaigns during that wilderness temptation. He did not go "off message" even when the Pharisees tried their best to lure Him away. Jesus maintained a certain consistency. So should we.

6. Frequency

I went to college with a guy named Paul K. Logsdon. We had a riot together in Communications classes and working at the campus radio station. Years later, when I had become a freelance writer, Paul managed a radio station in the East — and let me do bad celebrity impersonations on the air. Today he's the public relations director at our old college in Springfield, Missouri. Whenever I find myself in Springfield, Missouri, which is almost never, I look Paul up, and we have a blast together all over again. We're friends. Good friends.

Or maybe we're not.

Paul and I exchange Christmas letters — what his wife and kids are doing, what my wife and kids are doing — and sometimes actually even include a handwritten note in the margin! If I got in serious trouble, and Paul could somehow help from his perch in the college P.R. department, I imagine he would help me. And vice versa.

But what Paul and I have doesn't qualify as a deep friendship for lack of one critical component: *frequency*. When I pick up my phone and hear his voice, or show up in the doorway of his office, we instantly revert to 1974, Kraus Hall — it's like we never missed a day. But between those contacts, we have no relationship. *We have no influence in each other's life.* Neither of us brings anything to the other's world except fond, funny memories.

I would describe my friendship with Paul K. Logsdon as delightful. I would not want to give it up or trade it for anything. But it is not the kind of friendship with which I want to fill my life. My Paul K. Logsdon friendship is no match for my friendship with Phil Toole or Jeff Merry, each of whom I see three or four or five or twelve times a week. These are men with whom I am involved in work and ministry, whose families are intertwined with mine emotionally, socially, even vocationally. These are men who have watched me grow, and I've watched them. But more than that: we've participated in each other's growth. These are friendships that make a difference in my day-to-day life. *These are friends who influence me, and on whom I have influence.*

And it's this type of friendship on which we want to model our donor relationships. *Frequency* of contact is a crucial component.

> **℞** *Perhaps no other single issue has generated more anxiety in the ministry marketing meetings of which our agency has been a part.*

"We're mailing too much" is the refrain of ministry leaders, CEO's, managers, staffers, and board members. "We have to back off," they say; "people are sick of getting so much mail."

It's easy to understand how ministry personnel could get such ideas. They hear comments from their spouses at home, or a friend at church who happens to be on the mailing list. Or they simply look in their own jammed mailbox and arrive at the obvious conclusion.

But the obvious conclusion is very wrong.

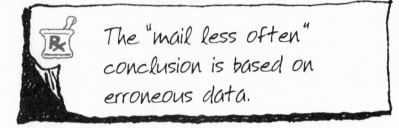

The "mail less often" conclusion is based on erroneous data.

A spouse's complaint or even a handful of letters from donors must be weighed against the dozens or hundreds or even thousands of positive responses — financial contributions — that your ministry receives in response to every appeal for help. Ministry personnel and their families tend to be on more Christian mailing lists than the average donor anyway, so the ministry staffer's own mailbox is a poor place to replicate the average donor's mailbox-emptying experience.

But even more dangerous is the significance we attach to a donor's letter of complaint about the volume of the ministry's mail.

"For every letter you get," ministry staffers have told me repeatedly, "there are a hundred or a thousand who feel the same way but don't bother to write. *They just stop giving.*"

But do the math. Let's say you have 10,000 donors. One donor writes to complain. This should mean that 1,000 of your donors never give to you again.

And that's only the Dark Side of the Force. Let's look on the bright side. You got a 3% response to your last appeal. That means, in essence, that 300 people wrote to *endorse* your mailing. Would you say for every giver there were another hundred or thousand who felt the same way but just didn't bother to send a check? You can't. You don't even have enough donors on your file to do the math.

Certainly it's possible that a single letter of complaint represents another individual, or another five, or another dozen who hold the same opinion. Even so, they probably don't begin to match up to the numbers of people who are supporting your ministry in response to mailing after mailing.

> We must learn to see a family member's complaint, or a letter-writer's complaint, for what it really is: one person's opinion — not the stuff around which we shape our ministry's entire marketing strategy.

But if you're getting an alarming number of complaints about the frequency of your ministry's mailings, should you just ignore them? No.

It is possible — maybe even *likely* — that your

mailings are not being perceived as valuable, helpful, or important.

Or perhaps every time you communicate with your donors, you're asking for something.

Either of these phenomena can produce a negative reaction on the part of your donors — but in such a case, the negative reaction occurs regardless of how frequently or infrequently you mail!

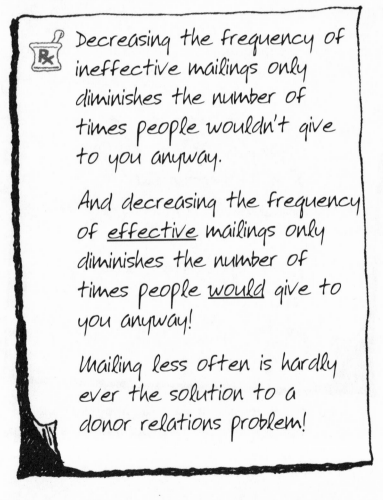

Decreasing the frequency of ineffective mailings only diminishes the number of times people wouldn't give to you anyway.

And decreasing the frequency of _effective_ mailings only diminishes the number of times people _would_ give to you anyway!

Mailing less often is hardly ever the solution to a donor relations problem!

Commercial advertising agencies have spent billions of their clients' dollars researching and proving the "principle of multiple impressions." In layman's terms, this principle dictates that a buyer doesn't buy the first time she hears the pitch. She hears it on radio, she sees an ad in the paper, she sees a commercial on TV, she hears it on the radio again, she sees a billboard, she sees a poster in a grocery store window, she hears it on the radio again — and finally she buys. Along the way, the light only dawns *slowly* — because along the way, she is distracted by the many other priorities of her life. Sure, you're amazed to see the same television commercial aired two or even three times during the same football game — but the research proves unilaterally that *multiple* impressions far outdraw an *individual* impression.

The principle of multiple impressions drives ministry marketers to two inevitable conclusions:

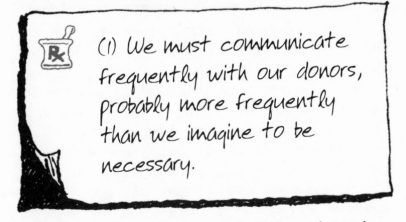

(1) We must communicate frequently with our donors, probably more frequently than we imagine to be necessary.

(The guy who makes Purina Cat Chow only needs one TV commercial to remind him to pick up some Purina Cat Chow on the way home — but then he's got a vested interest. It takes me about 14 TV commercials to get the same message — and even then my Siamese is usually whining with hunger before I actually make the purchase.

> **R̃x** (2) We must communicate the same message each time we communicate — because different messages don't add up to multiple impressions; each new message only qualifies as another initial impression! (See Deadly Disease #1: Amnesia.)

The more often you communicate a clearly defined mission, the more donors will understand it, internalize it, embrace it, and respond to it.

Friends stay in touch. They communicate often. So write often to your donors. Write as often as you have something to say. To the extent that your budget will allow, write sometimes without asking for money. (See "Quality" below.) Even appeal letters, if they're well designed and well written, will generate a positive visceral response from your donors. These donors have, after all, invested in your ministry; they are interested in seeing the work go forward. They have a certain demonstrated level of interest, perhaps even commitment. If you are writing as friend to friend — if you regard them as members of the ministry team, or family, and you reveal this in every communication — your donors will look forward to hearing from you.

If the leader or marketing director of your ministry lobbies for fewer mailings to donors, ask some hard questions:

- Are we thinking like the buyer, or like the seller?

- Do we imagine the donor's life revolves around the mail she gets from us?

- Are we engaging in wishful thinking, imagining that the donor vividly remembers the details of our situation from one mailing to the next?

- Are we tired of our own mailings — when the donor isn't?

- Is gift income going down, and we're cutting back mailing frequency because it's easier than figuring out what's wrong with our mailings?

Jesus modeled frequency for us. He ministered buckshot-style to the masses — but He zeroed in on those who had invested their lives in His work. His disciples and the women who supported them — these He devoted Himself to. He was in their faces again and again. It was only after an intensive three years of communication, of *relationship*, that He could physically depart and leave the work in their hands. Jesus understood the value of frequency. So should we.

7. Quality

Somehow, your best friend improves your life. He or she brings a certain quality to your existence. Your life is better in some way because of your relationship with that person.

Is your donor's life better because of her relationship with your ministry? Where ministry marketing consists exclusively of appeal letters, it's difficult to establish a feeling of "quality relationship" in the heart of a donor. The donor, after all, is being relentlessly asked for help. But there are ways to become a quality friend to your donors. Newsletters demonstrate the dividends of the donor's investment. Thank-you letters and thank-you calls deepen the bond of friendship. Give your donors gifts — insights, ministry products, whatever — that will improve their lives. Become valuable to them. Then they'll become valuable to you.

No, with this kind of approach to donor relationships, not every mailing can pay for itself. But if you continually build your relationship with your donors by a strategy of "quality exchange," the mailings that do generate a positive net return will more than cover the net-negative "quality" mailings in which you invested.

(The ugly opposite is also true: If you *don't* invest in

your donors, and you try to make every mailing net-positive, you'll find that your nets grow smaller and smaller — because a relationship with your ministry is less and less valuable to your donors.)

> **Rx** It is important to tell the donor what benefits she will acquire by responding to your appeal.
>
> Some ministry marketers shrink from this — they see it as bribery — but this view sadly misses the point.

At the very heart of the matter, every appeal you make to your donors is of benefit to *them* as well as to the ministry. It is, after all, good for people to give. God did not design us for receiving only; He designed us to continually pour out, so that He could continually pour in. If a person feels a certain warm satisfaction when she gives to a worthy cause, that's no accident — it's a reasonable after-effect of her functioning according to God's original design!

What this tells us as ministry marketers, however, is that there is always a benefit to the donor which can be pointed out to her when we ask her to give. The joy of giving is a very real thing, a valid benefit, and it should be made clear to the donor that she will experience it.

In many cases you may find that you can bestow additional blessings on the donor as she supports your cause — you can give a gift that expresses your gratitude and has some spiritual value to the donor — and this is legitimate, too. Offer a thank-you gift that springs from your own heart — an original book, an original booklet, a cassette tape, a collection of photographs with your own handwritten captions, whatever. But it's only gravy. The potatoes are more important: leading the donor to fulfill her calling as a giver to the work of God.

> You can say to your donors, in effect, "This is a good cause; give to it just because of that," without any reference to benefits the donor might enjoy as a result.
>
> But that's not even how Jesus operated.

He did not require people simply to give their lives to Him without any promise of benefits.

He *could* have, certainly. He might have chosen to walk the earth for three years just spouting platitudes —

totally true, eternally valuable — and who could have blamed Him? He didn't need to do a thing to prove Himself; He was the Son of God, with full authority therein, without a single sign or wonder, without a single word of corroborating testimony.

But He arranged plenty of signs and wonders, and plenty of testimony, "that you may be saved" (John 5:34). He opened His heart, healed the sick, raised the dead, mended broken hearts.

He didn't say, "You'll be in good shape in heaven; just do what I tell you, and hang on till you die."

He brought quality into people's lives.

So should we.

8. Gossip

If the term *entertainment* makes Christians nervous, *gossip* makes them crazy.

To be honest (see "Truthfulness" above), I use the term mostly to wake up the people attending my ministry marketing lectures.

Let's agree to define gossip somewhat loosely — as information the donor can't get anywhere else. (See? "Information The Donor Can't Get Anywhere Else" just doesn't have the *bite* that "Gossip" has.)

Any ministry in the world can say, "Here's what we're doing; please support it. And when you give, I'll send you this wonderful whatever ...." But only *you* can tell the story of a family touched and transformed by the love of God through your unique ministry. Only *you* can tell how your heart broke as you witnessed the crying need of an individual — and how your heart soared as you saw that life restored ... by the grace of God, through the generous giving of your ministry family. Only *you* can tell what God is doing inside your ministry, where He's leading you, what's on the horizon.

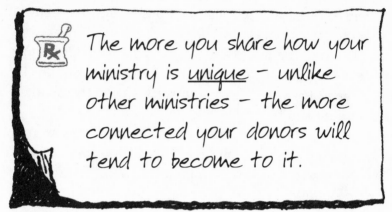

The more you share how your ministry is <u>unique</u> — unlike other ministries — the more connected your donors will tend to become to it.

If someone gives an initial gift to your work, and it seems to be the only ministry doing exactly what you're doing, the donor has little choice but to continue supporting you in order to support that type of effort!

Obviously this doesn't mean you run down other ministries in your communications with donors. (Besides being ungodly, it usually results in an ugly backlash.) But it does mean that you continually push to reflect the specific accomplishments of your ministry.

Let me meet the individuals impacted by the work.

Let me see the specific changes that have come about as a result of this ministry.

Take me behind the scenes, into your heart, into the hearts of those whose lives will never be the same because this ministry intersected with them at some wonderful point in time!

If I find myself inspired by such results, I have to support you — and keep on supporting you.

I had a friend who tried his hand at the travel business for a while. He stood up at a local Chamber of Commerce breakfast during the "networking" part of the monthly gathering where each member took a moment to describe their business.

"We're Such-and-Such Travel Agency," my friend announced. "We have all the bells and whistles ..."

What he was telling us was that his travel agency was just like a bunch of other travel agencies.

What he *needed* to tell us was *how his agency was different from all the rest.*

> ℞ The more generic your ministry communications are, the more easily your donors can turn to other ministries.
>
> The more unique your ministry communications are, the more easily your donors can grow deeply involved with your ministry.

Jesus turned His world upside down. Nobody else was saying the things He was saying. He was willing to risk losing some followers (and He did; just look at John 6:66) in order to establish *deep* and *lasting* relationships with the rest.

Jesus lived by this somewhat unorthodox definition of gossip: He offered something that people couldn't get anywhere else. So should we.

9. Relevance

Here it is — the Big Kahuna of friendship.

Here's where the greatest number of ministry trains leave the tracks.

Here's the most conspicuously absent component of friendship in the entire world of donor relationships.

Here's the subject I had a great big argument about, just yesterday, with our agency's Creative Services Director.

"Relevance," I said, "is the single most essential ingredient of a deep and lasting friendship."

"What do you mean by relevance?" she demanded.

"If you and I have a deep and lasting friendship," I explained, "then I have the feeling that it's about *me*, not about *you*."

"That's the most horrible, selfish thing I've ever heard," she grumped.

"It is not," I replied.

"It is too," she shot back.

"Is not."

"Is too."

Somehow I must have failed to communicate effectively.

But regardless of my clumsy work explaining the concept to our Creative Services Director, the marketing of your ministry must make the ministry *relevant* to the donor.

You may talk all about your organization, you may talk all about the specific needs you're facing, you may talk all about the lives that will be touched and transformed by God through your efforts, and you may ask me — *implore* me — to help you accomplish something important and wonderful ... but I will respond only to the extent that I see myself in the picture.

The appeal must be about <u>me</u>; it can't be just about you.

Remember James Carville (the "unjust steward" of our modern parable back in Deadly Disease #1: Amnesia)? He understood in that first Clinton campaign that the message must be expressed in ways that *make it count for the voter* — or, in our case, the donor.

The cause must involve me.
It must have some impact on my existence.
It must bring some dynamic into my life.
It must change me somehow.
It must alter the way I feel about myself.
It must bring a welcome adjustment of my self-view.

Does this seem selfish and shallow?

Yes, it seems that way.

But this is still how every human being thinks and operates. We're back to the concept of value exchange (see Deadly Disease #3: Neurosis and Character Disorder.)

Even if I am the most selfless, big-hearted, giving person on the planet, I am still regarding every opportunity for action ultimately in terms of its impact on me.

An example: my friend the late Mark Buntain was the Protestant Mother Teresa. He spent virtually his entire adult life in Calcutta, feeding hungry street children, building a hospital, a school, a church. His heart shut down before he turned 70. When he died, it was revealed that he had suffered from leprosy for many years, the direct result of his intimate daily sacrifice of love for the children of India.

Mark was perhaps the most selfless person I've ever known. Imagine spending decades doing the same difficult work as Mother Teresa while she got all the press! But did Mark Buntain regard every opportunity for action in terms of its impact on him? Yes. When he saw a need, how did he decide what to do about it? He may not have cared about his own pain and suffering, his own deteriorating health, his own discomfort — he may have been willing to do anything for the cause regardless of the potential negative impact on his finances, his reputation, his family — yet he had to ask himself, "How do I fit into the picture? What can I do about this?" Give him a situation where he could make no impact, and Mark Buntain quickly lost interest.

A Harvard professor quit his academic career to care

for a profoundly disabled friend. It appeared that the ex-professor had made the most selfless decision imaginable. And he had — except that he could tell an interviewer precisely how *he* had grown spiritually as a result!

I want to believe that I am completely selfless in my devotion to my wife Kristina. Sure, I want to please her because I love her — regardless of any benefit to me. But I cannot escape the realization that I am going to experience a burst of warm satisfaction when I walk through the door with fresh flowers and I see her eyes light up. I am fascinated by her, but I respond to her because of how delighted I am to be in the picture with her.

Relevance is the inescapable requirement each one of us places on every action we take. It has to be about us. I have to be able to make a difference, or experience an impact — or my interest is minimal.

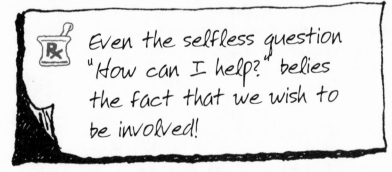

Even the selfless question "How can I help?" belies the fact that we wish to be involved!

How, then, does this phenomenon of the human psyche affect our communications with donors?

If I'm your donor, every appeal must be about me — not you.

I have to perceive a connection between the cause

and myself.

This is more than simply saying "Give and you'll accomplish this and that" — although this approach goes in the right direction.

Making the appeal relevant to me involves intertwining my own experiences and my own emotions with yours. E*specially* since I'm busy, bored, and a bad reader, the very *beginning* of your letter to me needs to be about me — to cut through all the noise I'm being bombarded with. If it's about *me*, I am enormously more inclined to take a moment and explore the proposition.

When you're a ministry marketer, writing to the donor about the donor is hard work. In my role as our agency's copy chief, I pass judgment on much of the copy we write for ministries, and our writers have grown to anticipate the first question I ask about every letter package: Is *the lead* (the first paragraph of the letter) *about me*? Sometimes it seems impossible to do — but when we realize that the reader is busy and not necessarily interested and subliminally considers reading a challenge, we go back to the drawing board and find a way to *connect* the reader to the appeal from the very first moment.

Here are some hits and misses from our own files:

> "The nightmare happening in Lawrence, Kansas, today could soon be happening in your hometown." (That's about me.)

> "Today the federal government is over $4 trillion in debt." (That's somewhat interesting, and only somewhat about me.)

"I am sending this important communication to you because our May 15 Matching Challenge deadline is fast approaching!" (That's not about me.)

"Where were you 35 years ago?" (That's totally about me!)

"Two hundred eighteen years ago, our Founding Fathers signed their names to a document that made them criminals." (Yes, but how is that about me? I might be enough of a history or justice buff to continue — if you're lucky. Otherwise, sorry.)

"You and I are not even safe in our own homes." (That's about me.)

"Our parents and grandparents came to this country from all over the world." (That's sort of about me, but only tangentially.)

"Do you believe Americans have a right to take a Bible to work with them?" (This is about me — because you want my opinion.)

"We are facing a crisis of character." (Aw, I dunno. Who's "we"?)

"I am alarmed and heartbroken to have to write you this letter." (Good transparency — I might be intrigued enough to go on reading — but it's not much about me.)

"If you've ever seen an unsaved loved one come to Christ, then you know how Alexander feels." (That's only vaguely, potentially about me.)

"Please read the enclosed fax I just received from Russia. It's from my son Ron, who directs our ministry campaign worldwide. He explains the situation in Russia and the Ukraine." (Yeah, but it's not about me.)

"The spring campaign is underway in Mexico — Children, teachers, families and entire communities are being impacted! We're strengthening local churches through our efforts." (But you're not writing to me about me.)

"You have been seeing the tragedy in Bosnia-Herzegovina on the evening news and reading about it in the paper ...." (This is only remotely about me.)

"What would you do if your *entire month's* salary wouldn't buy a month's worth of food for *one person* in your family?" (I'm with you. This is about me.)

"You've got the ticket in your hand — Passport in your pocket. The plane is powered up, and they're calling for rows 10-27 ... That's you."

(Wow! This is about me!)

If, in that first moment, as I read the lead of your letter, you make a connection to *me*, I am far more likely to open up a channel. The more intertwined we become over the course of the letter — the more I can see myself in your picture — the likelier I am to keep that channel open — where communication can occur, where persuasion can take place ... a path along which I may respond to your request.

If in that first moment there's no connection to me, you're making a huge assumption — that I'm fascinated by you, that I have time for you, that I feel some urge to stand with you. But those are definitions of the seller, not the buyer.

Even with my closest friend, when he comes to me and reports some wonderful exploit, I'm not delighted simply because of his success. My delight comes from the jumble of our mutual past and future: how we've interacted in the past, how I expect we'll interact in the future. I'm delighted by what happens to him because he's already established his relevance to me. (We can't assume our relevance to our donors because — remember? — they're busy, bored, and bad readers. Only the most loyal and generous donors — practically members of the board — can be trusted to see us as automatically relevant to them.)

If my best friend only *ever* reported his wonderful exploits when we got together, we wouldn't form a deep and lasting friendship. At best, we'd be a couple of those friendly acquaintances — or I'd be simply a "fan." Some ministry leaders seem to want fans instead of friends —

and some have more fans than friends — but fans don't last as long, don't get as much out of the relationship, and don't satisfy as deeply as friends do.

Jesus made Himself relevant to people. He started where *they* were and drew them to Him.

He met a woman at a well; He talked about water.

He was approached by Nicodemus, a man consumed with issues of bloodline; He talked about the birth process.

He could have made the Gospel a philosophical treatise and demanded that we memorize it. But He loved us enough to *relate* to us.

He put it all on our terms.

He practiced relevance.

So should we.

* * * * *

All of which is well and good — since most of us do these nine things when we communicate with our donors.

But there's more. And the road gets rougher.

Chapter 6

NEVER NEVER LAND

The hardest work is the most satisfying

If that's all it took to build relationships — just the nine phenomena we've explored — most ministries would have big donor files full of happy, healthy donors.

But there are five more components of friendship ... and they're the tough ones. The ones most often *missing* from ministries' relationships with their donors.

Here they are:

10. Entertainment

Godly people cringe when I use this term, but fear not: we're not talking about Howard Stern here. Entertainment is the phenomenon of being interested, intrigued.

> Friends stay friends in part because they find each other interesting, even amusing.
>
> Likewise, boring appeals never raise money.

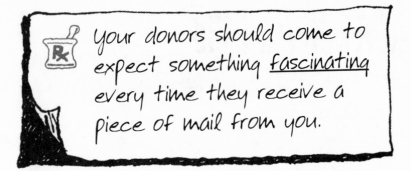

Your donors should come to expect something <u>fascinating</u> every time they receive a piece of mail from you.

Does this contradict the principle of consistency? Yes and no. You must maintain the same character each time you communicate with your donors — but you must vary your presentation enough to be interesting.

Here's what I tell ministry principals and marketing directors: Be an excellent writer. If you can't be, hire an excellent writer. (Not a *formal* writer — a *vivid* writer.) Mailing letters is too expensive to have donors yawning and dropping your appeals in the trash. Use active verbs. Coin phrases. Exclaim. Emote.

A letter to a donor should have life. Pep. Zing. Or drama. Or charm. Or bits and pieces of all of the above. If the donor comes to expect boring, low-energy communication from you mailing after mailing, the relationship is doomed.

This concept applies to more than the text of your donor communications. We find that when the *look* of a ministry's mailings vary from package to package, reader interest is heightened.

If you resist the idea of visually interesting graphic devices in your mailings, is it because you want to believe your donors are loyal enough not to "need" graphics? You may be thinking more like a seller than a buyer.

Do you dislike the idea of "eye bites" — short paragraphs, underlined phrases, narrowed paragraphs — which help the reader through the package? They tend to capture and hold the reader's interest.

> Would you rather your donors
> were so fascinated by your
> ministry that such devices
> couldn't increase readership
> of your appeals any further?
>
> I wish that were true. But it isn't.

Your donors, just like virtually all the Christian donors in the marketplace, need their interest to be *gained* and *held*. That's entertainment!

Entertainment also involves connecting with the emotions of a person. Emotion is absolutely crucial to the science of direct response.

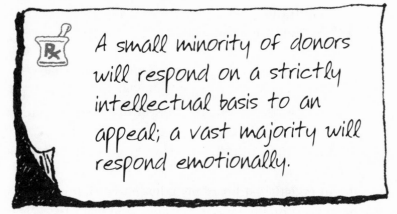

A small minority of donors will respond on a strictly intellectual basis to an appeal; a vast majority will respond emotionally.

Does this contradict what we've already discovered about *information*? No. This *balances* what we've already discovered about information. Omit information and your appeals are empty cheerleading exercises; omit emotion and your appeals are cold, clinical treatises. Neither generates maximum response.

It is extremely easy for a ministry to become boring to its donors because of that overwhelming "seller mentality": we fail to distinguish between being *fascinated* and being *fascinating*. In the same way, it is extremely difficult for a ministry to become entertaining to its donors. There are myriad obstacles to overcome:

the hard work of thinking up new approaches to text and graphic design for mailing after mailing;

staff members who recognize how much extra work it is to do something different each time;

the bias against entertaining because it contradicts our view of ourselves as sophisticated leaders;

a deep-down resistance to the notion that we *need* to be entertaining in order to make a connection (because we want to believe that the donor is eagerly awaiting our next communication);

and this list probably goes on.

In spite of the difficulties it causes to the seller, entertainment is crucial to connecting with the buyer.

Jesus was the Master Entertainer. He didn't do stand-up comedy, but He riveted the attention of His audiences with a variety of devices. He talked to them on their own level, about their own concerns, in their own language — and He pulled no punches.

Time and time again we read about members of His audience hearing His words and then trying to crown Him king — or plotting to kill Him.

Jesus got a response!

His words were vivid.

This is a clear symptom of entertainment.

Jesus entertained.

So should we.

11. Feedback

Friends listen. But ministries don't tend to.

Solicit feedback from your donors.

How is the organization changing their lives?

What kind of impact is the ministry making?

How can you make more of a contribution to their spiritual growth?

Ironically, the ministries that end up being "complaint-driven" — overreacting to a small number of complaints and changing direction accordingly — are often the same ministries which fail to solicit feedback from donors. They have no apparatus for donors to communicate with them as "members of the team," yet when criticism somehow makes its way to them, they respond to it as if it were an edict from on high. Far better to create some kind of regular device for donor feedback, which has the effect of bringing a broader and more representative cross-section of opinion to the surface — so the criticisms can be received in the context of the compliments!

You can make feedback a regular feature of your mailings, by including a section on the back of each response form for comments. Even better, ask for prayer requests and comments. Better still, ask your donor to tell you how God has worked in her life through your ministry. This kind of all-purpose "response opportunity area" on your response forms can benefit the ministry in three ways: by revealing areas of donor satisfaction or dissatisfaction; by giving the donor a heightened sense of "ownership" in the ministry; and by bringing to your attention true stories of individuals' lives touched — stories which can be shared later in some form as evidence of the ministry's effectiveness. (Back to the chapter on Schizophrenia!)

Jesus was not just a lecturer. He often drew people out with questions.

> "Why are you so afraid?"
> "Which is easier ...?"
> "Do you believe?"
> "Will you give me a drink?"
> "Why are you thinking these things?"
> "Why did you doubt?"
> "Who touched my clothes?"
> "Who do you say I am?"
> "What are you arguing with them about?"

"Why are you bothering her?"
"What do you want me to do for you?"
"How many loaves do you have?"
"What good will it be for a man ...?"
"What do you think, Simon?"

He made people part of a conversation — and by the time He got to the bottom line, they had already signed on ... they had already participated, taken ownership. They didn't always end up agreeing, but they had to respond!

Christ's encounters with the woman at the well, with Nicodemus, with Peter — each of these demonstrates a delicate conversational seesawing between the parties. Jesus brilliantly employed feedback — the constant eliciting of the other person's views, ideas, opinions, and emotions — in order to generate a response. So should we.

12. Transparency

Imagine your pastor keeping his wife and children at home — sending them to a different church — never mentioning their names, never referring to them in conversation.

Imagine him parking down the street, slipping in the back door of the church, never letting you know where he lives.

Imagine him never telling you a thing about himself, about his activities, about his feelings.

How effective could his ministry be?

The truth is that many ministers operate on this basis — and many churchgoers have come to expect it.

They sit in the pew, they listen to a sermon, it's full of truth, it's full of theory, it's full of instructions for them — but there's no connection to the individual delivering it. All of which is all right ... but not ideal.

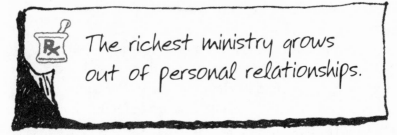

The richest ministry grows out of personal relationships.

    If my pastor is transparent — if I see how he actually *lives* what he teaches week in and week out — his words have far more impact with me.

    Even within the context of the sermon itself, personal transparency increases the listener's attention and retention. When I teach seminary students the principles of communication and persuasion, we confront the fact that churchgoers reflexively tune out about 20 minutes into a sermon — unless the preacher "interrupts" himself with an attention-salvaging device. One of the simplest devices is to reveal something about himself.

Because of the way human beings are wired, we respond to transparency.

    When you tell me something about yourself, it signals me that "we are alike" — and that opens a channel between us.

Likewise, one of the most powerful tools of communication available to a ministry marketer is simple transparency. When the ministry leader tells me, in the context of an appeal letter, something about himself, it engages me in a way that no amount of rational explanation of the need and the benefits can.

A letter to your donors might say, "I feel this is one of the most important actions we could ever take together." But it would more effectively communicate if it said, "I was sitting in my Buick yesterday, stuck in traffic. I normally would have been frustrated about running late, but instead I found myself thinking about this plan — because it's one of the most important actions we could ever take together."

You could ask me to give to a project — or you could tell me that you and your spouse have talked about it and decided, because you believe in it so strongly, to give a sacrificial gift ... and ask me to do likewise.

Transparency has a connecting effect on a reader or a listener.

"Yesterday my six-year-old said to me ..."

"When our dog ran away a few weeks ago, we thought ..."

"I hardly ever skip the sports section of the paper, but this morning ..."

For some reason, transparency makes us want to hear more.

Seminary students squirm in their seats when we get

to the transparency discussion. They are steeped in the Scriptures, consumed with the truth, and ardently wish to believe that the sheer veracity of God's Word, properly explained, will convince listeners. But this view misses one critical fact: the listener judges not only the message, but the messenger. It takes enormous discipline to separate the two. That's a discipline most donors can't be expected to demonstrate, particularly as they stand over their garbage cans reading our appeal letters, sitting in front of their TV sets fingering the channel button on the remote control, or reaching for the dial of the car radio.

Many ministers go through their entire ministry careers without revealing themselves; they may get away with it, but they haven't communicated as effectively with as many people as they might have otherwise. Many ministries establish large mailing lists with loads of donors without transparency — but they never know how much *more* they could have accomplished, how many *more* donors they could have inspired, how much more those donors might have given, if the ministry leader had been willing to be transparent. The more the messenger is intertwined with the message, the better able the listener/reader will be to receive the message.

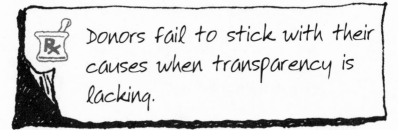

Donors fail to stick with their causes when transparency is lacking.

Here's how we put it in our somewhat famous "talking frog ad" which ran in national trade magazines and, I imagine, offended quite a number of ministry leaders:

> Most ministry leaders want to present a perfectly polished, corporate organization to their donors. So that's what they do. They present the organization, its goals, its activities — and not an ounce of their own humanity. The result is: their donors don't become their friends. Their donors simply give to the concept of the organization — and their loyalty never takes root. When another cause comes along — or, even more likely, a human being who establishes a real relationship and asks for help — that donor is gone.
>
> Next time you sign your name to an appeal letter, take a moment and read it through again as if it were going to your best buddy from high school. How would he or she feel about you, getting a letter like that? Chances are, you've written a corporate treatise — but not a letter from the heart.
>
> You'll never get the old man to kiss you that way.

Jesus revealed Himself to His disciples. He didn't hide. They saw what He was, day in and day out. Jesus expressed Himself transparently. So should we.

13. Vulnerability
This may be the most painful component of friendship — but it is the stuff the deepest bonds are

made of.

One of our clients tended to be quite closed in discussing his emotions; he was extremely reluctant to reveal anything of the sort to his donors. But there was a program produced by his ministry which was particularly close to his heart — a program designed to help underprivileged children in very practical ways. The ministry leader grieved, literally, over his ability to fund the program fully. But year after year, the donors failed to respond. Finally, he agreed to bare his soul. In a letter to donors, he admitted how deeply he was hurting about his failure to raise the money needed. He didn't whine; he just expressed the truth about the frustration and pain he was feeling — in the context of the children's need.

The results were powerful. Donors responded to his willingness to disclose his own pain. They gave generously. The program's funding increased dramatically.

Vulnerability made the difference.

Vulnerability takes transparency one dangerous step further: now, instead of simply revealing myself to you, I will reveal to you things that you could use *to hurt me.*

No wonder it's one of the five friendship components (maybe one of the *two*) most often absent from ministries' donor relationships.

Vulnerability opens the heart in ways that nothing else can. It says,

> "I have doubts,"
> "I have bad days,"
> "I get tired,"
> "I get angry."

Vulnerability takes huge risks — because the donor could easily respond with "I hate you for that."

But that hardly ever happens.

Instead — because vulnerability is so rare — the donor is astonished.

And because the risk you've taken is so evident, the bond between you and the donor is dramatically intensified.

"I wish I had done it differently." Could you admit such a thing to your donors?

"This situation has me more discouraged than I've ever been." Can you imagine your donors *not* reading the rest of a letter that began with those words?

"I had an argument with my wife yesterday, and..." That's vulnerability!

I have heard countless objections to the doctrine of vulnerability:

> "Aw, people don't want to hear about my troubles."
> "Our donors just want the facts — 'Tell me what to do.'"
> "This is fundraising, not psychotherapy."

Okay, I hear all of that. And no, vulnerability should not equate to the wanton airing of your dirty laundry. Your appeal letters don't need to become psychoanalysis-by-mail.

But where it's appropriate — where it helps your donor to understand your frame of mind, and why you feel something is important, or how you came to be in a certain position or hold a certain view — vulnerability can make a tremendous impact.

> **Real friends tell on themselves. Admitting to your own flaws is a sign of trust. Trust <u>connects</u> people.**

And if indeed the average donor fails to make much of a distinction between the message and the messenger, you *need* ways to connect to that donor — *person-to-person*, not corporation-to-facilitator.

In teaching settings, when I ask attenders why their best friend is their best friend, I often hear the word *trust*. "I can trust my best friend." But I don't include trust as one of the 14 components of friendship.

Why not?

Because when I quiz an individual about *why* or *how* they can trust their best friend, they always come to rest on one of the 14 components on the list.

Your friend is reliable? That's consistency.

Your friend is willing to be open with you? That's transparency.

Your friend never lies to you? That's truthfulness.

It's the friendship that generates the trust.

Over time, however, trust takes on sort of a life of its own. It greases the chute between the ministry's request and the donor's response. The donor doesn't have to be skeptical, doesn't have to be careful, doesn't have to inspect the appeal in fine detail, if trust has already been established.

> Generally, we observe that donors are quicker to trust ministry leaders than ministry leaders are to trust donors.

Yet practicing vulnerability in our communications with donors can become one of the most rewarding aspects of the relationship. Making oneself vulnerable has a certain cleansing quality — the feeling of "I have nothing to hide" is very freeing. You'll often get a warm response from donors when you've made yourself vulnerable, and that's enriching too. (In clinical terms, we might say vulnerability leads to feedback.) Vulnerability intertwines truthfulness and transparency, commonality and "gossip." It is, in short, the breathtaking extreme of a ministry leader's contribution to a relationship.

The story of Jesus' earthly life is a story of vulnerability. He wept; He squirmed; He admitted not wanting to go to the cross. Philip Yancey, in *The Jesus I Never Knew*, refers to what Dostoevsky called "the miracle of restraint." While at any moment God could squash any of us like a bug — and we would deserve it — He loves us so much that He *doesn't* squash us. Yancey observes that God "granted us the power to live as though he did not exist, to spit in his face, to crucify him." He made Himself *vulnerable* to us.

"Although power can force obedience," Yancey writes, "only love can summon a response of love, which is the one thing God wants from us and the reason he created us."

Christ's vulnerability is the ideal model for us.

When we make ourselves vulnerable to our donors, we say to them, "I am not going to manipulate you into responding; I am not going to try to overpower you and get you to do something you don't want to do. I'm on your level. I just know this ministry is doing good things, and if you become part of it, it will be good for you as well."

Jesus made Himself vulnerable even though He didn't have to. So should we.

14. Passion

And finally, passion.

Of all the components of friendship I've been able to isolate, here's the only one that isn't a requirement for deep and lasting friendships.

I have observed keen friendships which contain all the other 13 aspects, but which simply roll along pleasantly.

And that's okay.

But donor relationships are difficult to maintain without this component — because it is difficult to overcome the donor's distractions, apathy, and poor reading skills with anything *less* than passion.

People's lives tend to be average, unexciting. They may have a bright spot here or there, but by and large they are shuffling along day by day without many thrills. In many, many people there is something crying out for passion — for something to feel intensely about. They want to believe that there is something worth being passionate about — and if you speak passionately to them, they are likelier to open that critical channel of communication.

This is not to say that you have to pound a shoe on the table in your appeal letters. You do not have to pretend to be something you're not. But even a more rational, less emotional person at the helm of a ministry should feel a certain quiet sort of passion about his work — and that passion needs to come through.

Speak with intensity to your donors.

The power of words tends to fade on paper, so you can usually afford to crank up your letters.

If you write at 120% your usual intensity, it will be received in the reader's mind at about 80%.

Years ago I wrote fundraising packages for a major charity that helped hungry children. The leader of the ministry was uncomfortable expressing his emotions. He *felt* deeply — you could see it when he interacted with the kids — but he refused to let us represent any of that in letters to donors. As a result, the charity raised only a fraction of the support that it could have. The children received only a fraction of the help they might have.

Was I being unfair when I concluded that the ministry leader's problem was actually *pride*? To protect his own image of himself, he short-changed the children he loved so deeply.

I call this a case of misplaced priorities. Maybe I'm just a big bully.

Or maybe I'm right.

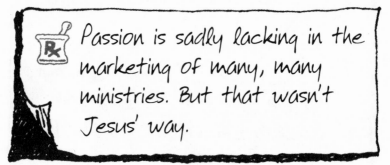

Passion is sadly lacking in the marketing of many, many ministries. But that wasn't Jesus' way.

Jesus felt deeply about His mission.

He used harsh, even slashing language; He wielded a whip.

He must have been fascinating to watch!

Even when He was telling recipients of His healing miracles to keep the news to themselves, He gave "strong" warnings. Jesus expressed Himself passionately.

So should we.

* * * * *

When we establish and cultivate friendships with our

donors, our ministry family grows, and grows strong. But when we fail to communicate on a friend-to-friend basis with our donors, we build an accidental Tala — we banish them forever to a leper colony, far from our midst.

If we wonder where our donors went, that's where.

We gave them a kind of leprosy ... and then sent them away ourselves.

Chapter 7

DEADLY DISEASE #5: MANIC DEPRESSION

Whoop-de-doo! (Sigh ...)

Sometimes fundraising is detective work.

After 20 years of raising funds for ministries, my ears are tuned for two suspicious statements:

(1) "Ya can't really raise much money for this kind of ministry" (which means that team members have somehow come to the conclusion that their ministry is too unusual, or too usual, or too low-key, or too complicated, or too simple, or too humble, or too lofty, or too something-or-other for people to embrace and support) and

(2) "This is a great ministry; everybody ought to be supporting it! Why aren't they responding?"

Both are honest expressions of the heart. But when I hear ministry personnel express either of these viewpoints, I put on my Columbo trenchcoat and start searching for bodies.

I'm looking for people whose lives have been directly impacted by the work of the ministry: someone who came to faith in Christ, a homeless woman who got a job, an abused child rescued and now thriving in school, a troubled marriage saved, a drug addict delivered, a suicide averted.

I'm looking for the success stories.

I search through the ministry's communications to its supporters, looking for stories of people whose lives are different because of the ministry.

If the ministry is actually accomplishing something of value, it is somehow helping people.

If a ministry is helping people but never lets me meet those people, the ministry has failed to capitalize on its single most effective tool for persuading me to be involved with the ministry.

If the ministry doesn't invest its energies in finding those "helped people" and capturing their experiences, only the tiniest fraction of such true-life testimonies will ever surface.

And if no such testimonies can be found, it means one of two horrible things: either (a) the ministry has no adequate apparatus for collecting such stories, or (b) *the ministry isn't really accomplishing anything in people's lives.*

Please don't let (b) be true; the answer must be (a)!

The vast majority of ministries have no apparatus at all for collecting success stories — I'll call them "testimonies" — because they do not understand the crucial importance of sharing them with donors.

Some ministry marketers, in fact, actually resist the use of testimonies. Maybe they've been turned off by the melodramatic weepers on late-night charity infomercials. But rejecting the use of testimonies on this basis throws out the proverbial baby with the bathwater.

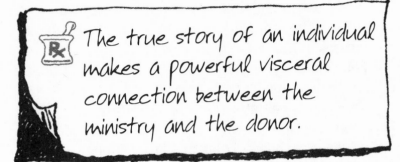

The true story of an individual makes a powerful visceral connection between the ministry and the donor.

I can relate to another human being — better than I can relate to statistics about thousands of people helped.

Even if the ministry masks the identity of the individual to protect his or her privacy, the sharing of that story gives the ministry a certain *credibility* that no volume of statistics or celebrity endorsements can duplicate.

In the shorthand of our agency, we refer frequently to SOTO — the Story Of The One. If we have a choice between starting an appeal letter with a true-life story or starting the appeal with *anything else*, we choose SOTO every time. The "story of the one" engages the donor's need for commonality, truthfulness, information, "gossip," entertainment, and most of all relevance.

> The average donor is far more interested in what happened to someone than they are in how your program works, or why.

For years Pat Robertson's Christian Broadcasting Network led the way in this field. In the late 1970's that ministry employed two fulltime staffers who did nothing but follow up on testimonies. Testimonies were valued so highly that any call or letter containing the germ of a testimony was funneled to these workers. They would write or call the individual, conduct an interview, and in some cases follow up with a camera crew. The most compelling stories wound up on the 700 *Club*, but dozens of less fantastic testimonies made their way into CBN's newsletters, appeal letters, and — perhaps most importantly — receipt letters. The personalized letter over Pat's signature which accompanied every donor receipt almost always included a brief testimony. Also in the receipt package was a "bounce-back" coupon — a generic response device designed to accompany another gift.

As a result of the ministry's consistent sharing of success stories — evidence of the donor's investment bearing actual dividends in people's lives — the receipt package bounce-back coupon came to represent as much as a *third* of the ministry's total gift income!

Down through the years we have seen only a handful of ministries devote themselves faithfully to the collection and re-transmission of testimonies.

> Rex Humbard's ministry used to produce "World Outreach Conferences" for donors, and a minicam was always stationed in a corner to capture people's stories.

> Cornerstone TeleVision in Pittsburgh has an aggressive testimony-collection operation.

Here's Life Inner City, the urban outreach of Campus Crusade for Christ, tracks down inner-city testimonies energetically.

Book of Life International sends volunteers on overseas "Affect Destiny" missions to give the *Book of Life* to schoolchildren in their own language. The ministry's "Affect Destiny" Team Director Rich Ryan instructs all of the ministry's volunteers to keep their eyes peeled for the story of a particular child whose life is touched by that ministry, and who touches a volunteer's heart. He urges volunteers to record the details, snap a photo, and write a letter to him when they get home. Book of Life's "Celebrations," gatherings of ministry donors, also feature testimony sharing-and-recording times.

But far more common are the helpless sighs of ministry personnel:

"We never hear about stories like that."
"We can't afford to put any of our staff on that."

In fact, a ministry can't afford <u>not</u> to pursue testimonies.

Without consistent living
evidence of the efficacy of your
ministry, you aren't inspiring
your donors as deeply as you could.

How can you systematically set out hooks and reel
in testimonies?

We often suggest soliciting testimonies from
donors in a more-or-less-standardized area of
the response form (the back, maybe?).

Media ministries can also establish an annual
"Letter Week" as a tradition, where you ask
people to share what the ministry has meant to
them.

Organizations which focus ministry on parties
outside the donor family, however — disaster
relief groups, child sponsorship organizations,
Christian schools, and so forth — have a
harder job.

They must make story-collecting a priority at
the "point of purchase" — where the ministry is
actually occurring.

Ask your disaster relief caregivers to write up or
phone in reports; give them a 24-hour phone
number to call, with nothing but a phone
machine on the end of the line.

Write to the caregivers who deal directly with
the sponsored children in your program and
ask for their impressions of outstanding or
unusual cases.

Get on a schedule of contacting each teacher in
your Christian school — maybe once a quarter?
— in hopes of hearing about kids making
extraordinary progress ... or about kids making
ordinary progress, but who couldn't have come
to school at all if it weren't for those donor-
subsidized scholarships.

The "story of the one" is important because so many
Christian ministries have "manic depressive syndrome" —
and the "story of the one" is good medicine for it.

What is manic depression in a ministry?

Well, some organizations are manic — they
communicate with high emotion, but not much
information — while other organizations are depressive,
communicating loads of informative data but without
much emotion.

As we have seen, there are numerous reasons for
ministries to be skewed one way or the other, but a
balance between the two is preferred.

The "story of the one" has the natural effect of
leveling out either extreme.

Say you're one of those ministry marketers more
inclined to raise money via emotion than information. We
see this often in ministries which have sprung from the
Pentecostal and charismatic traditions, and in quite a few
ministries dedicated to helping children with various

needs. Tell the "story of the one" in an appeal, and you've provided some substance — some hard evidence indicating that your ministry is actually accomplishing something with the donor's dollars. Not that you can use a story and abandon the use of hard facts altogether — but a testimony helps.

Or say you're one of those ministry marketers more inclined to raise money via information than emotion. You're just not comfortable expressing a lot of passion on paper; it's not natural for you. Tell the "story of the one" in an appeal, and you almost automatically heighten the emotional quotient of your package. Not that you can use a story and abandon the use of emotional language altogether — but a testimony helps.

Either extreme — manic emotionalism or depressive informationalism — undercuts a ministry's potential for building donor relationships.

But either extreme is also cause for concern because of what it may say about the *heart* of the ministry, its leader, and/or its marketers.

In some high-emotion/low-information ministries, I've observed a generally low opinion of the donor. The ministry's personnel treat the donors as if they're stupid — willing to respond to preposterous requests or a flimsy case for support. Low regard for the donor is a symptom of donor relations schizophrenia (see Deadly Disease #2).

More commonly we observe high-information/low-emotion ministries — and here we often find marketers who feel compelled to use *every* communication to tell donors *all* about *everything* the ministry is doing. In some cases this reflects a subtle, deep-seated pride: "This ministry is great, and I want her to know all about it." In other cases this urge springs from a feeling of insecurity about the relationship between the donor and the ministry: "I've got to overwhelm her with data because she's so skeptical, or even hostile."

In both of these scenarios, however, the ministry marketer fails to distinguish between being *fascinated* and being *fascinating*. He becomes like I was when my son Kristofer first arrived in our home: "Sit down, pour a cup of coffee, and I'll tell you all about my little boy. It will only take a couple hours — and then, if you have to leave, I'll continue on the subject some other time. Because, of course, my little boy is the most fascinating topic of conversation I can possibly imagine."

> Regardless of the marketer's motives of the heart, the donor does not want or need to know the details of the ministry's operation.
>
> How the ministry happens is not nearly as important to her as what the ministry accomplishes.
>
> We must paint the picture of results in her mind.

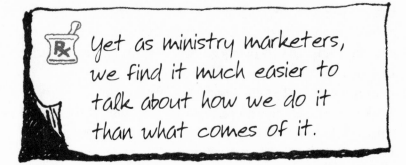

> Yet as ministry marketers, we find it much easier to talk about how we do it than what comes of it.

The "story of the one" takes far more work than the "story of assembling the food boxes" or the "story of building the school building" or the "story of getting on six more TV stations to reach a million more people."

Testimonies sometimes nicely bridge the gap between *what the ministry needs the money for* and *what the donor will sit still to learn about.* "We've got to book the hall now in order to prepare for the crusade." I don't care. Tell me about Lorraine, who was strung out on drugs but somehow came to Christ through the last crusade you staged. "We need new computers in order to process ministry correspondence and donations more efficiently." I don't care. Tell me about Patrick, to whom God gave a whole new life through our ministry, because someone like me gave generously!

There's some discomfort about the idea of raising money for "one thing" and spending it on "another thing." Certainly if you raise "designated" money for a specific project, you have a legal and moral obligation to spend the money on that project. But what if your ministry does three different things, but the only time your donors respond strongly is when you describe one of the three?

I have friends who have just such a three-pronged

ministry: they train worship leaders in a region of the United States; they minister through music and worship in a local church; and they adapt worship leader training for the unique cultures of various foreign countries. It astounds me that their donors respond most warmly to the foreign component of their ministry — it seems impossibly esoteric to me — but that's how it is. Their dilemma is whether to talk only about their foreign program in their appeal letters, or whether that would be fundamentally dishonest when more than two-thirds of their energies are spent stateside.

The solution is always to talk about *one thing* — and that's *somebody whose life is different today* because of your ministry. With that "story of the one," the mechanics by which that person was ministered to becomes less important to the donor.

> "Carlos has a safe Christian home today because friends like you gave to this ministry."

> "Debbie carried her baby and gave him up for adoption because friends like you gave to this ministry."

> "Sharon is a healthy, vibrant Christian today because friends like you gave to this ministry."

Never mind how your foster placement program works, how your crisis counseling center operates, how your intervention volunteers coordinate with the local police department. That's all well and good — but I want to *give* to your ministry because you told me about Carlos and Debbie and Sharon.

We often find that a ministry accomplishes seven or eight distinct functions, but five or six of them have no "sizzle" for fundraising. What to do?

I know of one honorable charity guided by leaders who insist on rotating through their various departments, appealing to donors to support each one in turn, and explaining in laborious detail how each outreach comes about. The ebb and flow of gift income is inevitable: some of the outreaches have far more pizzazz than others.

While some ministry marketers may believe that "equal time" is the only ethical route to generating support for their work, I have a contradictory view: I think it's completely *unethical* to cheat people in need — to do less ministry, or do it less well, for lack of funds — simply because each department of your ministry insists on its day in the sun.

> Tell your donors the story of someone whose life was touched and transformed by God through the work of your ministry, and <u>nothing could be more legitimate.</u>

We don't know exactly how Jesus and His disciples met their financial needs; those details aren't important. What we *do* know is how their ministry *impacted lives*. That's what's important.

It has often been pointed out that Christ calls us not to be His lawyers but rather His witnesses. The marketing of your ministry can be reduced to the same simple strategy. You can, in effect, let individuals tell "what happened to me" — and if what happened to them is good, you have an "automatic" instrument for inspiring people to help it happen again to others.

Put on your trenchcoat and make like a detective. Find the bodies. Tell the "story of the one." Let the evidence of your ministry speak for itself.

You've been charged with having an effective ministry. Can you be found guilty?

Chapter 8

DEADLY DISEASE #6: BLINDNESS

*There must be an ear of corn
here somewhere ...*

Years ago I managed a magazine for a major
ministry, and the ministry leader's wife would only let us
use black and red ink.

Ask me why.

I don't have a clue.

My predecessor in the position warned me not to go
proposing any blues or greens, or I'd only undermine my
position in the organization.

"How could you put up with this?" I groused.

"Count your blessings," he said with a shrug and a
wry smile. "Black and red are the best printing colors."

I wish to point out — with no small amount of
puffed-up pride — that before I left the organization four
years later we had produced a blue and green issue. (But
only one, come to think of it. After that, we went back to
black and red.)

I have a friend — who heads a ministry — whose
wife signs off on all the ministry's marketing plans. "Will
Mrs. Z like it?" is the final strategic question of every
planning session. Does Mrs. Z have an impressive array of
degrees in marketing? Does she have a brilliant track
record of marketing successes? Is she a major donor,

giving 80% of everything the ministry takes in — and making it reasonable to keep her happy?

No, no, and no way.

She's just the ministry leader's wife.

Looking across the ministry landscape, there's the incompetent brother-in-law, the megalomaniac daughter, the hard-of-hearing uncle ... these and many others, connected by blood or marriage to the ministry leader, assigned some task, and bringing their unique charm to the marketing process.

"No phone calls to donors."

"Full color in the newsletter looks too flashy."

"No photos of Dad without a necktie!"

"The newsletter has to be full color or it looks tacky."

"Two-page limit on appeal letters."

"No underlining."

"Okay, underlining — but not handwritten."

"Okay, handwritten — but only in black, never in blue."

God love 'em.

Somehow, they've managed to gain a foothold in the marketing of the ministry — control of the budget, or the purchasing of supplies, or the selection of thank-you gifts for donors, or the mailing schedule.

And in spite of however wrong they may be about whatever issue, they hold the reins.

The ministry leader — apparently appointed by God to lead the cause "for such a time as this" — defers to the judgment of someone else ... a ministry Rasputin ... one who holds some mysterious power over him.

And *that* one decides on marketing issues.

Of course, in other ministries, we find staffers

praying fervently for a mom or a brother-in-law or a
prodigal son to step in and bring some influence to bear
— because the ministry leader is so sold on his own
instincts. He's got a bad feeling about this technique or
that — personalized letters have a bad reputation with
him, or all response forms have to be identical. Or he
likes a certain look, and doesn't want to tamper with it.
And no amount of reasoning will move him off his hunch.
He is a seller, and utterly convinced that the buyer thinks
just like him.

This kind of rigidity is even more alarming when one
considers how many heads of ministries live in a
"bubble." David Kramer, in his bestseller _What It Takes_,
observed the bubble into which the President and Vice-
President of the United States are sealed as soon as they
take office — a bubble full of unique comforts, unique
pressures, and unique side-effects — and a bubble in
which they are trapped until they leave office. Living in
the bubble, it is virtually impossible for them to get in
touch with the way real people live (remember George
Bush being blown away by the marvels of optical
scanners in grocery store checkout lines?).

Ministry leaders typically become _consumed_ by their
work. Outside of the ministry, they don't have a life. No
"civilian" friends outside the ministry. Maybe no non-
Christian friends at all. They lose touch with how regular
everyday people think, feel, hurt — and how their
affections are swayed.

So they trust their own instincts (sometimes
hanging their opinions on God's influence, although it's
probably dirty pool to blame Him) — or they trust Mom's.
They feel they are leading a ministry, but in fact they are

flying blind. Circumstances are guiding *them*, not the other way around.

Does this description sound way too harsh to apply to you? Maybe so. But this seemingly honorable attitude of self-reliance — I call it donor relations blindness — manifests itself in a variety of symptoms.

Maybe you don't like the idea of being blind. Then again, you may have to admit that you have one or more of its side-effects.

Here are a few of them.

The test ban

This is not a nuclear arms treaty. This is a reluctance to test marketing packages or concepts before committing to use them with your entire donor family.

Perhaps the notion sounds too mechanical, too "Madison Avenue," for a Christian ministry. Maybe it sounds like a lack of faith to test an idea before using it unilaterally. But it can also be seen as a matter of good stewardship of your ministry's financial resources.

If you mail a package to your entire file and it only raises half the money you need, don't you feel guilty about the loss?

The leader of a ministry with over 100,000 names on its donor file wanted to solicit pledges of monthly support, something he had never done before. An agency helped him come up with a few ideas for a monthly donor program; he fell in love with one of them. Let's test the three strongest ideas on 1,000 or 5,000 names a piece, the agency said. No, he said, *this* is the winning idea. And he mailed that series of pledge recruitment packages to all 100,000 names.

Was it an act of faith? Or foolishness?

By God's grace, the campaign succeeded — at least the mailings didn't lose money. But no one will never know if the ministry *could* have generated 20% more monthly pledgers — or 50%, or 100%, or 200% more monthly pledgers — by mailing a different series of packages.

One of the great tomes of the advertising industry, *Tested Advertising Methods* by Robert Caples, begins with these words: "The effective strategies are tested strategies." Caples is legendary, and deservedly so, but he didn't just go into a trance and come up with brilliant stuff. He tested.

Likewise David Ogilvy, renowned for his brilliant creativity in advertising. The reputation, he admitted, annoyed him — because people seemed to miss the fact that *research* was every bit as important as creativity in the building of his advertising empire.

To the ministry leader who says, in essence, "I don't test; I just trust," I offer this encouragement: Testing doesn't reflect a lack of faith; rather, it reflects a sensitivity to your donor.

Testing recognizes that we may accidentally miss the mark and speak to the donor in a way she can't appreciate.

My high school French teacher, a dear friend with whom I've stayed in touch lo these 25-plus years, just revealed that she's going to retire. I want to go to the big bash, but it's 1,500 miles away. I could have just called my travel agent and booked the flights, but there are other issues: the cost of the trip, the loss of income while I'm away from the office, the burden of solo-parenting which I'll be placing on my wife Kristina while I'm gone. So I didn't just call the travel agent. I waited till dinnertime, then I floated the question:

"How would you feel about my going back to Indiana for Betty Weber's retirement party?"

That's testing.

The test failed, by the way.

Even as a failure, however, the test was a success — because my relationship with Kristina is none the worse for wear as a result.

When you discover you've mailed a "losing" package (or mounted a "losing" donor-calling test) to only 1,000 of your 20,000 donors, you have minimized the damage to your ministry and to your donor relationships.

Perhaps the most serious "damage" you've done to the donors who received the test is that you've cheated them out of the blessing of responding more generously to your need.

> Testing is the lost art of Christian ministry. It's shocking how seldom it's done.

We trust, we don't test. We say to ourselves, "*This* is really interesting!" Or, "That other ministry does it this way; so will we." Or, "God has given me this great idea ..."

We fly blind.

And when we crash, we wonder why!

Crumbs in the forest

Wasn't it Hansel and Gretel who tried to keep track of their whereabouts by dropping bread crumbs along the forest path — only to find that birds came along and absconded with their markers?

Later, if I remember correctly, they tried it again, but this time with stones — and found their way back just fine.

In our ministries, we need to keep track of how we got to where we are.

If we value our relationships with our donors, we need a system for tracking their responses to our requests for help.

This kind of information — the first cousin to testing — is superb for guiding our future interaction with them.

Here again, tracking is a natural dynamic of relationship. The next time I want to fly off on one of my, uh, *missions*, I'll have the benefit of remembering Kristina's loving, gentle, icy glare. Likewise, if you know that only half the usual number of donors gave gifts in response to your brilliantly conceived and executed "Parade of Presidents" appeal, you can set that "Parade of Presidents" idea aside as you plan for the future.

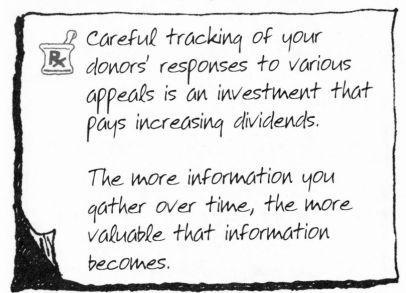

Careful tracking of your donors' responses to various appeals is an investment that pays increasing dividends.

The more information you gather over time, the more valuable that information becomes.

Technology is easily available today which tracks an amazing volume of detail — not only appeal by appeal, but *donor by donor*. Each donor's individual record can contain a history of responses — each with each item "sortable." This means you can isolate all the donors who gave, say, over $25 to, say, more than three appeals over the course of, say, the past 12 months.

Let's say your ministry helps people recover after natural disasters, but also operates a Christian school, as well as a bunch of other stuff. You can isolate all the donors who have responded to your disaster relief appeals but *not* to your scholarship appeals. The power to sort with such flexibility allows you to speak to donors more and more specifically.

To relief-oriented donors, you can send a version of your next scholarship letter which says, in essence, "I know you have a heart for disaster relief, but today I need you to help someone who's been stuck in an *everyday* disaster ever since kindergarten ... a young person trapped in poverty, who can't afford to come to our school."

Better yet, *test* such an approach on a small percentage of your file. You may find that it's better stewardship of your financial resources *not to ask* your relief-oriented donors to support your scholarship appeals.

This is the equivalent of how your pastor and staff deal with the people in your local church. They ask parishioners to volunteer for various jobs — teaching children, organizing social events, whatever — according to their own individual gifts, preferences, interests, and experience. It makes complete sense for my pastor to say to me, "Doug, you've done so well directing our drama ministry in the past, would you like to be involved in putting together some radio promotions for our church?" It makes far less sense for him to invite me to be involved in refurbishing the foyer. (What's this stuff? Sandpaper? What's it for?)

By the same token, if I ask a donor to get involved in a project that she has already rejected repeatedly, I'm signaling that I don't really know her or appreciate her as an individual. Tracking her responses enables me to grow more intimate with her as a person, as a member of my ministry team.

"Last year you did me the favor of giving $35 to our summer teen workshop campaign, and I loved seeing what God did through your generosity and the generosity of so many others. Would you be willing to give $35 to our summer teen program again this year — or maybe even $40?"

Compare the power of this request — the feeling of *relationship* that you get as you read it — with its evil generic twin:

"Every summer we ask our friends to help us produce teen workshops. I loved seeing what God did through the generosity of so many of our friends last year. Would you be willing to give $35 to our summer teen program — or maybe even $40?"

Not only is the generic request much duller than the personalized one; I also run a risk in asking for a specific dollar amount, because $35 might be far more — or far less — than the donor has demonstrated a capability of giving.

Research shows definitively that asking for a specific dollar amount generates a higher level of response than simply asking for "a generous gift" (people want to be told specifically what they're being asked to do), but asking for a specific dollar amount is problematic or impossible without adequate *tracking*.

> If our goal is to connect with our donors where they really are — spiritually, emotionally, financially — we have to capture and continually

update as much information
about them as possible ... in
the same way that we, quite
naturally, capture and continually
update personal information
about our own friends and relatives.

On the grand scale of a ministry's marketing effort,
however, this means *technology*.

In some ministries we find a certain resistance to
new technologies. "That's not what we're about," some
say. But a reasonably powerful computer system and
basic "donor management software" are as important to
today's ministry as a telephone is to the local church. No,
you don't use a phone in the church service itself — but
obviously it's valuable for keeping in touch with the
church family, and for keeping the operation of the church
going.

Imagine a pastor who could only interact with his
people in person, in the church building, or by mail! So it
is with computer hardware and software in the life of a
modern ministry. A good donor management program can
provide a clear snapshot of your donor family.

We strongly recommend to our clients that they
invest in both an audited financial statement, which
shows where the money is going — and regular donor
management reports, which show where the money is
coming from, and why. Both tools are important to
achieving the best possible stewardship of the financial
resources God has entrusted to you.

No new Q's
In our neighborhood when I was a kid, we used the

phrase "No new Q's."

It must have been unique to Griffith, Indiana, in the early 60's, because I've never found anyone else who recognized the term.

It was a mean-spirited thing: If some of us were playing together and other *undesirable* kids showed up, we'd holler "No new Q's!" to signal that the game was closed — no new participants would be allowed.

Why did we do it?

Because we were foolish, cruel, insecure, power-mad, insensitive, selfish.

Even at such a tender age, we were, in our own way, dedicated to the status quo.

We were children.

In ministry, obviously, hollering "No new Q's!" would be crazy. Of *course* we want new Q's. We want lots of new Q's, and we want them to give generously.

Yet in the organization of our ministry operation, we actually shut out new Q's.

We do it accidentally, blindly.

How?

We devote enormous energy to accomplishing the work of the ministry itself (this is good); we devote somewhat less energy to cultivating relationships with our existing donors (okay, maybe the case can be made for that); and we devote *little or no energy at all* to identifying and recruiting *new* donors (oops — big mistake).

Many ministry leaders want to believe that their work is so exciting that people automatically want to get involved with it. Some feel constrained just to let God bring across their path whatever new donors He desires for them. But this wasn't the pattern Jesus promoted: He was an activist recruiter. "Follow me," He told His disciples-to-be. He *found* the healed paralytic in the temple. When He was looking to make an impact on people, He went where they were, He got in their faces.

We, too, must work at acquiring new friends for our ministries. The art of "new name acquisition" or "prospecting" is worth an entire book of its own — if not an entire library. Here, however, let's just say that prospecting is as essential to the future of your ministry as brushing is to the future of your teeth. Ministries that don't prospect *dwindle*. It is a simple fact of math.

> Donors get old. Their income can decline. They can die. Some can be lured away from you, believe it or not, by other interesting things to give their money to.

There are plenty of reasons why donors may leave you, and generally only *two* reasons why they may *join* you:

(a) they accidentally fell into your path and fortunately loved you, or

(b) you did the hard work of finding them, introducing yourself to them, inspiring them, and winning their participation.

The roots of prospecting need to grow deep down into your organization, in much the same manner as your testimony-acquisition effort. Whenever leading personnel from your ministry interact with Christians who aren't part of your donor family, those personnel need to have a prospecting device in operation.

For example: does your ministry leader speak in local churches? Let him ask the host pastor if he may distribute a postcard which makes it convenient for his listeners to request a free quarterly newsletter.

For years, Dr. Richard Dobbins of Emerge Ministries in Akron, Ohio, has successfully prospected with an even simpler device: he writes his own name, address, and phone number at the top of the first page of a yellow lined notepad, then asks his listeners to pass the pad around and sign on if they want the ministry's free newsletter.

Media ministries have a huge advantage but seldom make good use of it. A pamphlet can be offered on the air for free — or for any gift to the ministry. If the product is related to an issue the ministry deals with regularly, anyone who requests it has identified herself as a potential participant in your ministry, simply because you and she have a common interest.

(To keep your current donors from swamping the ministry with requests for the product, send it as a surprise gift to current donors in advance of the on-air offer. Size it to fit in your receipt envelope and let it ride with all receipts for 30 or 60 days before the offer begins; this will get it to most of your most faithful donors.)

Prospecting can also be accomplished through a wide variety of other means: staging special events, running ads in appropriate publications, "cold calling" via telephone, even renting mailing lists.

Almost invariably, prospecting is difficult, tiresome, and expensive work for ministry personnel. (Odd birds like me *love* it.) It is time-consuming to create a prospecting strategy, execute it, analyze the results, make appropriate changes, execute, analyze, change, execute, analyze, change. But it is enormously rewarding when you see new names appearing in your ministry family, and new donors emerging to help you continue your work!

It is crucial to recognize that prospecting almost never generates immediate revenue.

Today's economy dictates that it costs more money to acquire a donor than the donor will give initially. But prospecting is not intended to be a get-rich-quick scheme. It is, in fact, slow. It is an investment. Each donor acquired will bring a certain amount of revenue into your ministry over his lifetime. That "lifetime value" (excuse the crass phrase) is the crucial number, for it guides you in deciding how much you can spend to acquire a new donor. Here again, however, it takes a good tracking system to reveal the average lifetime value of your current donors.

Time warp

My seven-year-old daughter, the family police officer, is long on justice and short on mercy. Someday she will be a union negotiator, but in the meantime I am taking it upon myself to teach her to respect other people's points of view.

"Natalie, do you understand what I mean by *point of view*?" I asked her the other day.

"No."

This didn't surprise me.

"Well, if I look at you, I think you're little."

"I'm not."

"Well, I'm bigger than you, so from my *point of view*, you're little."

"I am not."

"Just listen to me, Natalie. If Katie Ogdon looks at you, you're big."

"I *am* big."

"Well, Katie's only three years old, so when she looks up at you, she thinks you're big."

"She's right."

"That's Katie's *point of view*. See? Different people can see the same thing, but have different *points of view*."

Natalie sat silent, scowling at me. I sighed. Had I gotten through?

"Dad," she finally responded, "that's just your opinion."

Hmm.

Oh, well.

I've met a fair share of ministry leaders who share Natalie's perspective: "I'm big, and if you don't see it my way, that's just your opinion." They are sellers, and they think buyers think just like them.

But this fails to take into account the phenomenon of *point of view*. And if I direct a ministry but rely only on my own instincts — or my second cousin's — or if I fail to track my donor's responses, I am very likely to make some significant blunders in my interactions with donors.

I'm likely to believe, for instance, that my donors and I are moving through time at the same pace. If a donor gives only twice a year, I imagine her saying to herself, "Hmph! I'm only giving to those fellas twice a year!" In reality, that donor sees herself as intensely loyal to the ministry — "I support that ministry," she'd say if the subject came up in conversation with a neighbor — and has no idea that she's only giving twice a year.

One of the people I admire most in the world is Bob Hoskins, founder of *Book of Life* International. This ministry takes the Book of Life — a harmonized gospel — to schoolchildren in their own languages all over the world. Bob is a giant of a personality, a model of righteousness, fearless and articulate and innovative and energetic and all the things I want to be. I have written for his ministry for more years than I have even known Dale Berkey. And of course, I support his ministry financially. I get Bob's appeal letters in my mailbox at home just like any other donor, and I respond faithfully. Generously. Almost every time. Well, most of the time. Actually, I guess, sometimes I throw them away, but ... But hey, I *love* that ministry!

In fact, when our agency created for Bob a letter package designed to gently nudge donors who had failed to give for 12 months in a row, I couldn't fathom the ministry actually *needing* such a letter. Imagine coming to know such a wonderful ministry, being involved, investing in the ministry, learning about how God is using the Book of Life in children's lives all around the world — and somehow failing to give for 12 months in a row!

And then I got the letter myself.

I shuddered as I read the gentle, almost apologetic words: "If our records are correct, we haven't had the privilege of your financial support for more than a year now ... and we really do need your help. If we've done anything to offend you, I sure want to hear from you, so I can make it right ...."

Ack!

I couldn't believe it!

As much as I love Bob, and as much as my heart supports that ministry, I had managed to go an entire *year* without giving. Each appeal letter had arrived in my home, and I had been either too busy, or too broke, or too distracted — or I had set it aside, telling myself I'd write a check "tomorrow" — or whatever.

Bob's point of view? I had gone a year without a gift.

My point of view? I'm a loyal and devoted supporter of the Book of Life!

> ℞ Donors don't track time the way ministry personnel do. A donor can give once in 18 months and still think of herself as a good and loyal doo-bee.

What does this tell us?

It tells us, among other things, not to write off lapsed donors. Our agency's testing of "renewal" packages sent to lapsed donors demonstrates clearly that lapsed donors have extremely high potential to become active donors!

Some ministry marketers are reluctant to remind a lapsed donor of her lapse. But such a reminder can be delivered with great care and love, completely in keeping with the character of the ministry.

An inquiry into the donor's needs ("Perhaps you've been facing some difficulties I'm not aware of") or an acknowledgment of the donor's priorities and prerogatives ("I know how easy it is to get busy with other things") can actually _connect_ the ministry leader and the donor, rather than _separate_ them.

We encourage ministries to write to lapsed donors and ask them to share their needs so that the ministry staff can support them in prayer — regardless of whether the donor is able to give again or not.

We also suggest testing various strategies for communicating with donors who have lapsed for as little as three months — and again at six, 12, 18, possibly even 24 months or later.

Of course, it is possible to carry this approach to the opposite extreme and _never_ move lapsed donors out of the ministry mailstream.

> It is disturbing to contemplate the enormous waste of financial resources reflected in a marketing strategy which sends the same appeal letter to both an active donor and to someone who hasn't been a donor for four years.

The donor's self-defined status as a member of the ministry family must be acknowledged in the language of the letter — or the ministry accidentally reinforces the idea that it's actually just a big mailing machine.

This same principle suggests that we should salute donors on the anniversary of their partnership with us. Even the simplest donor management software enables you to write to me and say, "Doug, you've been a part of this ministry since 1993, and I'm grateful." This kind of affirmation deepens my affection for the ministry, and makes me want to do more.

Guide dogs

We don't naturally want to need help. This, in fact, is the hangup a lot of people have with Christianity! We want to be self-sufficient. In our ministries, we want to be able to do it all ourselves. At worst, we want to be able to hire employees to do it all.

Sometimes that works. But in today's world of mass communications, marketing is a difficult and risky science, a highly specialized and volatile field of study.

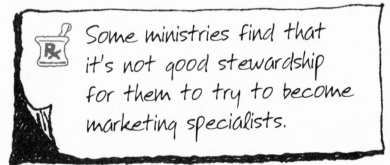

Some ministries find that it's not good stewardship for them to try to become marketing specialists.

It is more efficient for them to work with experts — ministry

development specialists whose
job is to find ways of integrating,
without compromise, the
character of the ministry with
effective marketing strategies.

It is risky to write about the wisdom of using
ministry marketing agencies from this vantage point —
senior partner in a ministry marketing agency. But the
truth is the truth, and I'll take the risk. Maybe you don't
feel blind enough to need a guide dog. But think about
how much *more* helpful a guide dog could be for a person
who can see!

A few days ago I interviewed a blind woman for an
appeal package I was preparing to write. She was tired;
she had been through a series of challenges — not the
least of which was adjusting to a new guide dog. The
woman had been blind all her life. Humans outlive dogs.
So from time to time, she's had to go through this
uncomfortable process.

It's not easy to start getting guidance from a new
source. One of the toughest adjustments is switching
from your mom to a marketing agency. But the results can
be terrific. And if they're not, well, there are other dogs.

* * * * *

A horse wears blinders because without them, it can
be distracted, even spooked. The trainer doesn't want
anything worrisome to come into the animal's field of
vision.

Frankly, I don't want anything worrisome to come

into my field of vision either. I would like my world to be carefree; I would like all my ideas to be brilliant; I would like to be right about everything. So I wear blinders. I do my best to shut out opposing opinions. I do this instinctively, effortlessly.

But I am not a dumb horse. I am in ministry. I have a higher calling. And the unpleasant truth of my life is this:

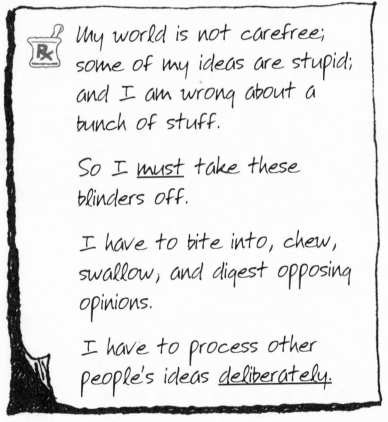

My world is not carefree; some of my ideas are stupid; and I am wrong about a bunch of stuff.

So I <u>must</u> take these blinders off.

I have to bite into, chew, swallow, and digest opposing opinions.

I have to process other people's ideas <u>deliberately.</u>

Bummer.

But only when I take in the whole horizon — only when I open myself to a panorama of viewpoints — can I be confident of settling on the *best*.

"Many advisers make victory sure," Proverbs 11:14 says.

I wish it didn't.

Proverbs 11:14 means I need to tune in to my donors' feelings and opinions, I need to go out and find new friends instead of just letting them find me, I need to see what the experts have to say about my situation — a whole bunch of stuff I don't want to do.

But it will be worth it. My ministry will grow. People's lives will be better. The vision God gave me will take shape before my eyes.

And that will be very good.

Chapter 9

DEADLY DISEASE #7: HARDENING OF THE ARTERIES

Thanks, but no thanks

Dale Berkey is on the road, away from home, three to five mornings out of practically every week. Yet no matter where he wakes up, he spends the first 20 minutes or so of his day running. It can be a blistering hot August morning in Phoenix; he pulls on some workout shorts and his footwear and off he goes. It can be a glaze of January ice and a vicious Chicago windstorm; he zips himself into a silvery sweatsuit — something that looks like bad science fiction — and off he goes.

He never skips a day, never makes an excuse. He can be sick, he can be tired, it doesn't matter; he's like a machine. He runs absolutely every morning.

Dale runs — and avoids red meat, and observes any number of other regulations and rituals — because he wants to see his son Blake grow up. Heart trouble runs in Dale's family, and Dale doesn't want any part of it.

If there are angels of death and one of them is assigned to do heart attacks, hardened arteries, and other ailments of the circulatory system, that poor angel must look at Dale Berkey and sigh wistfully. There's no way heart trouble is gonna get anywhere *near* this guy.

Sad to say, heart trouble also runs in my family. Not my physical family, but my professional family.

Look at the ministry marketing world — the somewhat strange, arcane, invisible world under the surface of the ministries themselves — and you find countless people like me.

We're ministry marketers, men and women with the rather odd task of soliciting and collecting money from people in order for our ministries to continue.

Day after day, we're more or less focused on one thing: getting a response of financial support from donors.

By the very nature of the work, our sensitivity to other aspects of our donors' lives — for example, how they're doing as human beings — tends to diminish.

We don't often think about what the donor is going through day by day — her health, her problems on the job, how she serves in her local church, her family pressures.

We just think about whether she gives, and how much, and how often, and how recently, and how soon she will again.

We get a kind of "hardening of the arteries."

We forget to be grateful.

The arteries of many ministry leaders get hardened too. They get caught up in the work of the ministry — achieving the goals of spiritual response, if not financial — and without realizing it they glide into a realm of insensitivity to their donors.

It's no small coincidence that Dale Berkey — the impresario of heart attack prevention — also diligently promotes the expressing of gratitude to donors. In spite of two decades in which Dale has been submerged in the world of direct-response marketing for ministries, he has somehow never lost sight of the fact that the donor is a human being.

When *Christian Management Report* asked Dale to write an article about thanking donors, the manuscript he submitted began with these wise words:

> "When you drink from the stream," the Chinese proverb recommends, "remember the spring."
>
> Christian organizations drink continuously from the stream of their donors' generosity. Sadly, however, we rarely remember the spring — the sacrifice represented by that $20 or $35 or $100 gift.
>
> The gift we receive so casually may come from a heart full of hurt: a mother agonizing over her youngster's schooling ... a grandfather troubled by his declining health ... someone whose own church is struggling financially ... someone who must decide between putting a check in the mail and giving a birthday gift to a beloved niece.
>
> Or that gift we receive may simply come from hard work — long hours in a machine shop, or late nights waiting tables.
>
> Or it may be scraped from the bone of a pension check, the pale reflection of a *lifetime* of work.
>
> In any case, it's not money we somehow deserve.
>
> It is simply money that God by His sovereign grace prompted someone to send

to us.

We need to remember the spring.

We need to say thanks.

Sure, our ministry goals are worthy. Our cause, Christ's Kingdom, is the greatest. Our dedication to the cause is commendable.

But, as Dale puts it, in the midst of our passion for ministry, we "tend to blast past the donor. *We've got her gift; now move on.*"

We fail to express to the donor how deeply grateful we are for her action, her sacrifice. In many cases, this failure is honest — because in fact, we're *not* grateful. We've developed hardening of the arteries.

There are both practical and spiritual repercussions to this.

On the practical side, we increase the risk of losing that donor. We are very likely shortening the lifespan of our relationship with her.

On the spiritual side, we are falling short of God's ideal.

Scripture doesn't simply challenge us to *feel* gratitude, but to *express* gratitude as well. Paul the apostle focused on this. He expressed gratitude to the Philippians, the Colossians, the Thessalonians, to Timothy and Philemon.

With the Corinthians he observed how gratitude becomes the happy side-effect of generosity.

"This service that you perform," he wrote in what might be called a "collection letter" to the Christians at Corinth, "is not only supplying the needs of God's people but is also overflowing in many expressions of thanks to

God" (2 Corinthians 9:12).

I've seen ministry leaders and marketers blanch when we suggest (as I did in Deadly Disease #2: Schizophrenia) that some components of a ministry's marketing strategy should be designed to express gratitude for results achieved rather than to break even or make a "profit." Gratitude, we suggest, can be regarded as an investment.

But many ministries take a compartmentalized view of their work. They require — and this seems honorable — that each and every function of the operation (each mailing, each product, each event) meet some kind of return-on-investment standard.

As they do, they are accidentally busting a principle which Jesus taught in one of His strangest parables — the one about the "unjust steward," recorded in Luke 16:1-13.

In this story Jesus salutes a conniving heathen — and for what? Reforming? No. For conniving!

Jesus actually made the crook into the hero of the story because he was wily enough to take _losses_ in the short term if it meant achieving _gains_ in the long term.

"The spiritually shrewd ministry manager of today

understands that sowing and reaping occur in *seasons*," Dale Berkey says, "that a wise investment of gratitude today pays off in a valuable donor relationship over the next year — or decade."

* * * * *

A brief aside about slow money.

It is not terribly unusual for ministry leaders and marketers to want success *fast*, as opposed to slowly.

Who could blame them?

But many good things in life are like Heinz, "the slooooow ketchup." You either take your time, or you settle for an inferior hamburger.

We see this conflict particularly in the area of estate planning, or "legacy income."

Ministries stand to generate a significant amount of revenue by motivating their donors to bequeath a portion of their estate to the ministry. There's a massive transfer of assets from every generation to the next. Over $3.5 trillion is sitting in retirement accounts alone.

But many ministries never invest in the establishment of an estate planning effort. Even now, when agencies like ours have developed strategies for accessing legacy income cost-effectively and with little risk, ministries drag their heels — preferring to focus all their energies on *money now*.

(This is doubly tragic because we've found that many ministries can not only recover their planned giving program investment within just 12 months, but also generate immediate money for operations along the way — even while they're building the organization's endowment for the future.)

Furthermore, many who *do* pursue estate planning devote most of their energies to finding that one mythical megadonor — the equivalent of winning the lottery — rather than committing themselves to the drudgery of inspiring *many* donors to get involved. David Henschen, talks about hunting elephants and hunting rabbits.

> You can live just as long on rabbit meat as elephant meat — but rabbits are easier to catch.

"Don't invest all your resources in hunting elephants when there are rabbits all around," David says. "We've seen way too many ministries spend way too much time and money looking for The Big One — that one fantastic donor who can plop down a million bucks. Yes, the elephants are out there, but it's far easier, and more efficient, to find the 10 loyal donors who can leave you the residual of their estate — often yielding more than $100,000 each."

Here once more, as in so many facets of our walk with Christ, His principles of life — like sowing in one season to reap in the next — turn out to be the most profitable. Our errant tendency is to look first for the profits. Somehow, the scriptural principles of life — like gratitude and patience — often get missed along the way.

* * * * *

Some ministries today are so out of touch with the idea of gratitude for donors that they don't realize which actions signal gratitude and which actions signal ingratitude. Yet some of the simplest functions of a ministry can communicate thankfulness to donors. Take, for instance:

> • **Putting a thank-you note in with the receipt, and getting it back to the donor as quickly as is humanly possible after her gift is received.**

Our agency has found that there is literally no single more effective way to lengthen the lifespan of your relationship with a donor.

How long does it take your ministry to get a receipt to a donor? A week? Too long. A month? Horrors. What are you saying to your donor by dragging your feet? "Ah, sure, you gave, but it didn't mean all that much to me."

> • **Acknowledging a suddenly-bigger-than-usual gift from a donor.**

If someone gives a gift half again as big as she's ever given, you have to believe she was somehow especially inspired — and she has probably made a significant sacrifice to give you that much. If you say a generic "thanks," well, that's better than nothing. But a warm note that acknowledges her special effort — "I couldn't help but notice how generous you were" — will go far toward deepening her connection to you and your work.

The same idea should apply whenever a monthly

pledger increases her monthly pledge, even slightly. That's a major signal of donor loyalty, and needs to be applauded!

> **• Calling your most generous donors, just to say thanks, because they are, after all, the people most responsible for enabling you to do what you're doing!**

Have a staffer or a volunteer call each of your top donors — just once or twice a year. Not to ask for help. Not to hint around about an upcoming project. Just to say thanks. Maybe to ask if there's a specific way you could support the donor in prayer.

> **• Dropping a handwritten thank-you note from a staff member or volunteer.**

This is the licked-stamp version of the phone call idea. "A handwritten note of thanks from a volunteer or staff member can make a powerful impact," Dale Berkey observes. "It can also make an important impression on the one who writes the note! What would happen if each member of your ministry staff began each workday by writing one short note of thanks to one donor?"

> **• Mail an annual letter of thanks instead of an appeal letter — no request for help,**

**no reply form or envelope
— to the entire donor file.**

How could you survive financially, since you couldn't expect a lot of donations in response to such a letter?

Break your mailing list into 12 parts, and mail the thank-you letter to one-twelfth of your donor family each month over the course of a year.

**• Send a note something like
this to every donor once a year
at the appropriate time:**

Hi, Larry and Joyce,

Just a note to say thanks.

It's been 3 years since you first joined with me in this work, and I am really grateful.

You've truly made a difference during this time — and I can't wait to see what God will do through you in the years to come as we continue working together!

Drop a line if you get a minute.

Yours in Christ,

Dave

**• Show your donor how her
investments are paying off by
inserting a leaflet in the receipt
envelope which shares the true
story of someone whose life has**

been impacted by the ministry.

(Berkey calls this _increasing the "gratitude power"_ of the receipt mailing.)

> • **Give a gift to your donor,**
> **without prior notice,**
> **without fanfare, with**
> **no strings attached.**

Not necessarily a big expensive gift. Maybe just a booklet, a tape, anything that comes with a brief note of thanks.

The fact that you sent it at all is more important to the donor than how much you spent on it.

> • **Help your biggest donors**
> **understand that they are leaders**
> **in your ministry by sending**
> **them an advance copy of**
> **any product you're going to**
> **be offering to the whole**
> **ministry family.**

"I'm going to be sharing this with our whole ministry family next month," you can say in a cover note. "But because of the major investment you've made in this ministry, I wanted you to have it in advance, as an expression of my gratitude."

> • **Build gratitude into**
> **every communication**

with your donors.

Don't eliminate or undercut the urgency of an appeal for help. But acknowledge to your donors that they have certainly helped to bring you as far as you've gotten.

* * * * *

Losing touch with the donor's humanness is dangerously easy to do.

We naturally tend to think of our own ministry as the most sensible place for anybody to invest. We forget that God entrusted that money to that donor, and she has a responsibility to Him, not to us, to be careful with it. She can invest it anywhere — and like it or not, many of those other options would reap just as valuable a harvest for the Kingdom as if she sent her contribution to us.

If every ministry leader and marketer got hold of this concept and actually lived and worked by it, we would see a lot less of the distinctly non-Christlike competitiveness that so alienates one ministry from another.

> TV preachers fret over other TV preachers siphoning off their market share.

> Local pastors bite their nails about new churches setting up shop in the neighborhood.

> Relief ministries sweat out the rise of other relief ministries (God forbid our hurricane package should get into the mail a day later

than _their_ hurricane package, for fear someone
might let _them_ help the hurricane victims instead
of us).

It never occurs to us that God's ideal timetable
might include a time of recalibrating for our own ministry
... a time in which we drop back a gear, and take stock of
our own spiritual health. Imagine God's will allowing for
another ministry to surge to the forefront! (Such a thing
could _only_ be temporary — couldn't it?)

It is difficult to confront the truth about the gift of
leadership — that it's an undeserved, unmerited gift given
by God on His own terms, in His own time, for His own
reasons. I'd like to think God made me a teaching pastor
at Mountain Valley Community Church because I'm such
hot stuff — so intelligent, so charming, so brimming with
insight. But it ain't so. He just decided to make me a
teaching pastor.

God gave you your unique ministry on the same
"divinely arbitrary" basis.

Facing up to such a frightening concept flies in the
face of an "I deserve this" attitude about the donor's
response to my appeals.

It also up-ends my spending decisions.

How do I spend the money my donors send me?

Am I using all of those God-given financial resources
to feed myself, to make myself look better, to climb the
ladder of the marketplace?

Or is there a part of my ministry which is devoted to
the needs of others, particularly those less fortunate?

One of the most enriching spiritual disciplines for
any ministry is to devote a portion of its own hard-earned

income to the care of others — outside the realm of their own ministry's operation.

Take, say, the equivalent of one month a year — a twelfth of all your ministry's income — and designate it for a completely unrelated ministry.

> A ministry which produces a television or radio program can support a neighborhood ministry to the homeless.

> A stateside ministry can give to an overseas outreach.

> A literature ministry can be a blessing to a feeding ministry — and vice versa.

This is a practice in which our agency has engaged for years, with Dale Berkey spurring us on. Dale sees to it that the agency supports not only our own client-ministries, but also ministries which are not our clients — particularly evangelistic and compassionate works.

Such a concept is hopelessly radical for many in ministry leadership. We are trapped by a persistent attitude of "How much will it net?" Our single-mindedness is admirable — it's all for the sake of the ministry, we tell ourselves — but our admirable single-mindedness eventually hardens the heart. We detach from the painful realities of other people's worlds — those of our own donors, as well as of people beyond the sweep of our own ministry. We get tunnel vision, and in the tunnel, everything is about us; nothing is about anything or anybody else. Committing ourselves to sacrifice, to giving something away — something we need, something that we could do a lot of good with — helps us see out of our tunnel.

"But we're struggling to make ends meet!" the ministry leader counters. "We're devoting ourselves completely to what God has called us to do — and we're already doing without for the sake of the ministry."

True, and you are to be saluted.

Unfortunately, however, this sounds strangely reminiscent of Isaiah 58:4-12, where God's people were doing more or less what you're doing — devoting themselves to God's calling, and doing without — and still winding up competing with each other.

In their situation, their devotion to God was expressed through fasting — yet their fasting was ending "in quarreling and strife, and in striking each other."

I see here a picture of well-intentioned ministries pursuing their God-given missions but jockeying relentlessly for position in the marketplace!

On the heels of this unpleasant assessment, the Lord speaks through Isaiah to offer a different approach:

> "Share your food with the hungry ... provide the poor wanderer with shelter — when you see the naked ... clothe him ....

> "If you spend yourselves in behalf of the hungry and satisfy the needs of the oppressed," He adds, "then your light will rise in the darkness, and your night will become like the noonday."

Is your ministry struggling?

It could be that a healthy dose of generosity is in order — perhaps the same kind of sacrifice you'd like to see your donors make on your behalf.

In our ministries, we tend to operate on the basis of the maxim that ministry follows money.

If I *can make a certain amount of money*, we say to ourselves, I *can minister*.

In God's economy, however, the opposite is true: If I can accomplish a certain quality of ministry, God will provide the resources to fund it.

Money follows ministry.

Can we live like this? Can we take such a concept — so dramatically contrary to the world's norm — and build our ministries around it?

I don't know.

It may take a leap of faith.

But it will surely — pardon the expression — pay off.

* * * * *

My uncle Rob in Chicago has always enchanted young children — which is good, I guess, since he had five of his own. The youngsters of his church have always flocked around him Pied Piper-style.

But Uncle Rob has never cultivated friendships with

children by the traditional methods — candy and gum, presents and surprises.

Instead, he uses quite an unusual alternative device. He uses *work*.

The first time I witnessed this strange phenomenon, I was nonplused.

"Hi, what's your name?" Uncle Rob asked, crouching down to reach the child's eye level.

"Andrew," the little boy answered.

Uncle Rob wasted no time.

"Andrew, I left my Bible in the front row," he said. "Would you please go get it and bring it to me?"

Andrew was gone in a shot, and quickly returned with the prize.

"Thank you, Andrew!" Uncle Rob crowed. "You did a great job! What a great worker you are!"

And the boy wandered away in a haze of pride, beaming in his newfound friendship.

Then Uncle Rob saw me staring at him. I'm sure my gaping jaw tipped him off.

"You don't make friends by doing things for people," he grinned. "You make friends by getting people to do things for *you*."

At first I thought he had a jaundiced view of life. But gradually I came to realize that Uncle Rob was actually applying a very sound scriptural principle.

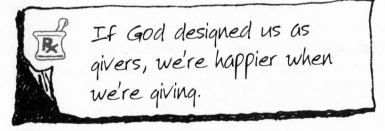

If God designed us as givers, we're happier when we're giving.

The world is full of takers — people striving to *acquire*. They get their cars and houses and careers and trophy-spouses and cute children all lined up, and then wonder why they don't feel fulfilled.

But people who learn to *give* are people who experience fulfillment.

"Give, and it will be given to you," Jesus said in oft-quoted Luke 6:38. "A good measure, pressed down, shaken together and running over, will be poured into your lap. For with the measure you use, it will be measured to you."

It's when we're already full that we can't receive any more blessings.

In this spirit, we can appeal to our donors with enormous love and caring. Richard Perry, a senior partner with the Domain Group, has written brilliantly and sensitively about giving's spiritual importance *to the donor*.

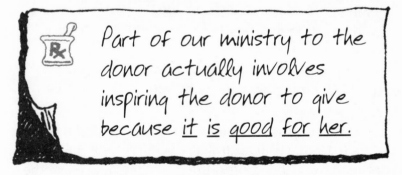

Part of our ministry to the donor actually involves inspiring the donor to give because <u>it</u> <u>is</u> <u>good</u> <u>for</u> <u>her.</u>

Philippians 4:17, which I've already quoted, is worth quoting again. In it, Paul explains his motive for requesting financial help: "Not that I am looking for a gift, but I am looking for what may be credited to your account."

Cynicism comes easy, especially in the business of marketing ministries. We could tell ourselves that the donor benefits by giving, and (heh-heh) so do we. So sell her the benefit — promise her the blessing — and reap the reward.

But somehow I don't think that's where Paul's head was as he wrote to the Christians at Philippi.

By the time he got to Chapter 4, where he talked about their financial generosity, he had already written Chapter 2 — and squashed the idea of selling "God's promise of blessing" for selfish gain.

> "Your attitude should be the same as that of Christ Jesus," he wrote. He "made himself nothing, taking the very nature of a servant." He "humbled himself and became obedient to death — even death on a cross!"

Not exactly the future I want to envision for my ministry!

And Paul goes on, as if we could possibly have missed the point:

> "... Become blameless and pure, children of God without fault in a crooked and depraved generation, in which you shine like stars in the universe as you hold out the word of life."

Yes, it will help the donor spiritually if she learns to give liberally. But not if she learns to give out of selfish motivation. We have a responsibility to cultivate in our donors the same love of giving that Christ demonstrated

— a willingness to sacrifice, even if it only meant growing closer to the Father.

When we lead our donors down that path — not only by our words, but by our example — our ministries will be stronger, healthier, more effective ... and more fulfilling for us to be involved with.

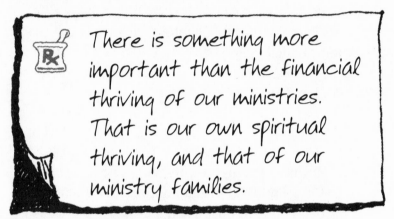

There is something more important than the financial thriving of our ministries. That is our own spiritual thriving, and that of our ministry families.

God did not design us as ministry leaders and marketers first, then as His children. He dreamed us up to be His children, and some of the joy of being His children comes from being involved in ministry.

I want to be so committed to a warm, open relationship with my Father that I'm willing to do anything to preserve it ... even if that means I have to set aside my ministry.

Is that too extreme?

Well, maybe.

But Jesus actually gave His *life*.

How extreme was *that*?

Chapter 10

POST-OP DIAGNOSIS

Where does it hurt?

Many people avoid medical testing because they don't want to know how sick they are.

The courageous ones look illness in the eye.

Are you feeling brave?

Here's the diagnostic checklist:

AMNESIA

Symptoms: ministry personnel can't articulate the ministry's mission in a single sentence.

(A completely healthy ministry knows who it is and where it's going, and communicates with its donors accordingly.)

SCHIZOPHRENIA

Symptoms: the ministry's marketing effort is developed apart from the ministry's mission; it may even drive the ministry's mission. And workers' roles overlap, with significant confusion and friction between areas of specialization.

(The healthy ministry's marketing strategy grows out of its ministry calling, not the other way around ... and the organization operates on the basis of a "community of specialists," with workers' functions sensibly and clearly delineated, so that each worker in the organization has a good handle on his or her proper role in the ministry.)

NEUROSIS/CHARACTER DISORDER

Symptoms: viewing donors as "just like us" or disdaining them as inferior.

(A healthy ministry sees its donors for who they are, and communicates with them accordingly.)

LEPROSY

Symptoms: treating donors like robots or cogs in the machinery of the ministry, instead of developing a friendship with them.

(The healthy ministry treats its donors with love and respect, cultivates relationship with them, and communicates with them accordingly.)

MANIC DEPRESSION

Symptoms: attempts to raise funds on the basis of information alone or emotion alone, instead of communicating the life-changing substance of the ministry's work.

(The healthy ministry invests significant resources in the collection of true-life "testimonies," and raises funds largely on the basis of true-life stories of individuals whose lives have been touched and changed through the ministry's efforts.)

BLINDNESS

Symptoms: developing marketing strategies on the basis of hunches or the instincts of self or close acquaintances, without a basis in reality.

(The healthy ministry recognizes that genuinely good marketing principles are biblical principles, and employs them appropriately.)

HARDENING OF THE ARTERIES

Symptoms: cynicism, with virtually exclusive emphasis on asking for help, and little or no emphasis on thanking or becoming a source of blessing to the donor.

(The healthy ministry invests significant resources in thanking its donors, recognizing them as crucial members of the ministry family.)

There's no shame in being sick ... only in rejecting the cure.

Jesus came for the goofed-up, He said in Mark 2:17, not for the got-our-act-together crowd.

The last thing I'd want to do is communicate any kind of condemnation. God works His wonders through imperfect instruments all the time. If He can accomplish anything at all through someone like *me*, He's amazing!

But everyone can benefit when one member of His body stumbles across a shred of practical truth and shares it with all us fellow-stumblers.

Over the years, we've stumbled, picked ourselves up by God's grace, and tried again to get down the road with His help. Why did we stumble there? In exactly that way? What really happened?

We've tried to ask ourselves the hard questions, turn up truthful answers — and share them here ... for the benefit of all the ministries God has raised up in our midst.

Our Lord has foreseen and made available the cures for all seven of the Deadly Diseases of Ministry Marketing.

These sicknesses are curable.
That means they qualify as

unnecessary distractions to
your ministry's mission.

Our prayer is that you will have the joy of complete
health in your ministry ... that you will experience the
freedom of "throwing off everything that hinders"
(Hebrews 12:1), every flaw "that so easily entangles," so
you can "run with perseverance the race marked out" for
you.

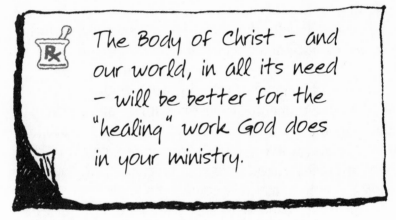

The Body of Christ — and our world, in all its need — will be better for the "healing" work God does in your ministry.

Could the treatment begin today?
The patient decides.

The end

Berkey Brendel Sheline is a "ministry to ministries" founded in 1983 by ministry development specialists E. Dale Berkey, Ph.D., and Doug Brendel. Along with partner Jack Sheline, this unique agency has helped a broad range of Christian ministries to fulfill more of their God-given potential.

Along the way, Berkey Brendel Sheline has successfully produced direct mail, prime-time specials, radio and television programs, telephone strategies, banquets, college admissions programs, large-donor solicitations, new name acquisition and upgrade efforts, capital campaigns, books, display ads, brochures, on-air spots, press releases, publicity packages, public relations campaigns, special events, corporation and foundation research and proposals, banquets, conferences, Internet sites, and more.

The agency has had the privilege of helping child-focused ministries and child sponsorship organizations, church planting ministries, colleges, universities, seminaries, denominations and denominational-focus ministries, ethnic-focus ministries, evangelism ministries, humanitarian aid organizations, international missions and outreaches, literature ministries, local churches, ministries to the disabled, substance abuse programs, television and radio programs and stations, urban and inner-city ministries, youth-oriented ministries, and still others.

Berkey Brendel Sheline has consistently maintained an open-book policy, inviting any interested parties to ask client-ministries directly about the agency's work. A list of ministries served by Berkey Brendel Sheline appears at the agency's website, www.servantheart.com.

"We've succeeded in working with many ministries

who could never seem to make it work with 'consultant types' before," agency president Dale Berkey observes. "We have long-term relationships with ministries because we have long-term interest in ministry. We don't send you a consultant. We make you a friend. We stand with you as members of your ministry team. We believe in accountability, the same kind of mutual respect that flows through any healthy family."

The cornerstone of Berkey Brendel Sheline's "ministry to ministries" is "The Code" — a dramatic commitment which has made a major impact in the ministry development realm. "The Code" is expressed in the agency's brochure like this:

We help ministries grow.

But we have our limits.

Because we live and work by a code.

The code is very simple.

It's two words.

The two most difficult, most powerful, most riveting, most compelling, most damning, most infuriating, most under-used, most fragile, most hopeful words in all of fundraising:

Be honest.

Honesty isn't always easy. Sometimes the truth hurts.

Yet honesty has its own rewards. You sleep better, if nothing else.

In fundraising, the story is the thing. Tell a good story, raise a lot of money. Question is, Is there a good story to tell? Or do we have to make one up?

Berkey Brendel Sheline made a decision long ago. We don't make stuff up.

We are privileged to serve alongside some of the

finest ministries in the world. We chose each other for a variety of reasons. But all of our clients share one common quality.

The stories we tell about them ... heartwarming, heartbreaking, faith-inspiring stories ... are true.

These are ministries who actually do what they say they do.

Is this a big deal? Yes, it is a very big deal.

In a world where scandal is only page 3 because it's so commonplace, Berkey Brendel Sheline takes the old-fashioned view.

Honesty isn't the best policy. It's the only policy. "Whatsoever things are true ... think on these things."

We want to help ministries grow. But we have our limits. A ministry may be wonderful, it may do great things, it may be world-famous. It may double our billings.

But we can't change our code.

Those two simple words are the words we work and live by. Words we consider more important than "Grow big" or "Hurry up."

If you agree with the code, we'd love to talk with you about growing your ministry. If you don't agree with the code, well ... we'd love to talk with you about why not.

BERKEY BRENDEL SHELINE
Ministry Development Specialists
60 Shiawassee, Suite G • Fairlawn, OH 44333

voice (330) 867-5224 • fax (330) 869-5607 • email servant@servantheart.com

www.servantheart.com